SADDLE FITTING

A GUIDE TO METHODS AND SOLUTIONS FOR THE WESTERN SADDLE

By David A. Prevedel

Copyright: David A. Prevedel, 2012

All Rights Reserved

No part of this book may be reproduced in any form whatsoever, whether by graphic, visual, electronic, film, microfilm, tape or CD recording, or any other means, without prior written permission of the author, except in the case of brief passages embodied in critical reviews and articles.

ISBN 978-1-105-53299-3

First Printing

TABLE OF CONTENTS

PREFACE

Chapter One - GETTING STARTED
    Priorities 1
    Does Your Saddle Fit Your Horse? 2
    Things to Check First 4

Chapter Two - OVERVIEW OF SADDLES
    Pieces and Parts 5
    The Saddle Tree 6
    The Seat 9
    Saddle Weight 12
    Gullet Width 13
    Saddle Riggings 14
    Rigging Positions 18

Chapter Three - SADDLE FITTING GUIDE
    Step One - Check Gullet Height and Width 22
    Step Two - Check the Bar Flare 23
    Step Three - Check the Clearance on the Shoulders ... 26
    Step Four - Check Rigging Position
        1. Bridging 27
        2. Not Enough Rock 28
        3. Too Much Rock 28

Methods for Checking on Bridging and Rock 28

Chapter 4 - SOLUTIONS FOR SADDLE-FITTING PROBLEMS

The Three-Way Rigging 35
Modifying Rigging Position
   1. How to do it 38
   2. Working Examples 40
Modifying Rock of Bars 54

Conclusion 62

Appendix 63

About the Author 69

PREFACE

Saddle fitting is far from an exact science. Some have even described it as confusing and over-whelming even for experienced riders; while others have called it a myth, great in theory, but impractical in the real world. By compiling what is known to work with some common sense and practicality, this book is an effort to give riders enough knowledge on the basic concepts to determine if their saddles are fitting properly. We will also discuss remedies that are available to correct existing problems; and for those who are a little more skilled, some actual saddle modifications.

There has been a long evolution in development of the western saddle. Saddles come in many shapes and sizes with different functions and utility that have changed over the last 150 years. It is common knowledge that horses do not have the same size and shape of backs. Like us humans, they come in all shapes and sizes: tall and short, wide and narrow. This occurs naturally in horses and selective breeding programs have also developed horses with vastly different backs. Thus, when we put saddles on these horses, coupled with the riders' various shapes and sizes, it is logical that some horses will develop sore backs and other complications.

Further compounding the problem is that horses cannot talk. It is up to us, as riders, to determine the degree to which the horse is uncomfortable, in pain, or just plain miserable with our tack.

There are many techniques and theories on saddle fitting. Many custom saddle makers and manufacturers provide measurement tools and templates to entice you to purchase a new saddle made to the measured specifications. This is a viable alternative, but an expensive one. However, for those of us who cannot afford a custom-made saddle, we typically purchase and use what we can afford, or use what we have and make adjustments.

It is a fact of life that many good horse riders are not saddle makers, and many good saddle makers are not good horse riders. Therefore, barring the theory that a little knowledge can be dangerous, our goal here is two fold:

    A. If you intend to purchase a new saddle off a show room floor or a catalog auction, what you should know about the chances that particular saddle will fit your horse, and

    B. If you have a saddle(s), used, new, or recently purchased, and know or suspect your horse is getting sore, what you can do about it.

Chapter One - Getting Started

Priorities

Many of us, when we acquired or purchased our saddle(s), never went through any evaluation process. We had no idea if a particular saddle would fit our horse. Generally, we looked at the price, the padded seat, the attractiveness, what is in style in the neighborhood or local arenas, and then we sat in the saddle to see if it was as comfortable as our favorite TV chair. Meanwhile, our poor horses waited in the corral for our "enlightened" purchase and good intentions. So now, let's look at taking this task a little different in the following priorities:

A. Priority One: Fitting the Purpose

There are many types of saddles specific to a particular purpose or use. The purpose can define style, swell shape, horn types, cantle size, and several other variations. Saddle types include roping, show, cutting, barrel racing, reining, pleasure, ranch, trail, endurance, and rodeo competition. Regional variations in type, such as the Wade, also come into play. New styles are continually being developed such as treeless, flex-trees, and endurance saddles. Although there are trade-offs in how these saddles appeal to the various riders, if they fit the purpose for which they were designed, then the rider(s) should be satisfied. The real question is how a saddle addresses the following three objectives: (1) Does it fit the horse? (2) Does is fit the rider? and (3) How does it distribute the weight of the rider on the horse?

B. Priority Two: Fitting the Horse

As would be suspected, this priority is the most important in assuring that sore backs of horses and other problems do not arise. It is the most difficult to assess, is often ignored, and can lead to very unhappy experiences and high costs. The majority of this booklet is devoted to this topic.

C. Priority Three: Fitting the Rider

Rider comfort is important, but note this priority has been placed last. The rider's poor posture, improper leg position, or poor weight distribution can affect the saddle fit and cause soreness in horses. Elimination of rider movement in a saddle is important.

There are several other variables or options to consider. Some of the more prevalent are seat length, seat padding, and even color which may fit the rider's fancy. Weight of the saddle is often the major consideration, not to mention cost fitting the rider's pocket book. How much the rider weighs is also important. Because the saddle must distribute the rider's weight on the horse, the bars and even the saddle skirts provide the contact area for weight distribution. Larger bars with good contact are necessary for heavier riders while lighter riders can get away with smaller bars and less contact.

Does Your Saddle Fit Your Horse?

So you think your horse has a sore back. As a start, we can generally group saddle-fitting problems and sore-back horses into two categories:

1. Problems that are of various theories and consequences that have no basic solution and will keep coffee-shop talk going for decades, and

2. Problems that can be addressed with common sense and are most likely correctable. Naturally, we will concentrate on this one.

If a horse has a sore back, it becomes a "detective hunt" to find the culprit. Saddle fitting is far from easily undertaken and your horse cannot talk or testify. How the saddle fits a horse was probably the last criteria you used when you selected your saddle. By human nature, we look at appearance, padded seats, and perhaps colors. Not until we get home do we find there are problems. And then the problems do not occur until the horse has been ridden under saddle. Most western stores and saddle shops do not have a "ride and try it" policy.

A horse with a sore back will have areas that are tender to the touch and will try to pull away or cringe from touching or pressing on the back. When saddled, some horses will balk, buck, try to rub the rider off, or just bear it and get sorer. Eventually the tell-tale white marks will begin to show as the hair follicles over the sore areas die, and are replaced with white hairs lacking pigment. Try the following:

- Touch and press on the horse's withers, along the backbone, and over the kidneys to see if the horse reacts to pressure in any particular area.

- Watch for uneven sweat marks. Sore areas may show large wet areas when the saddle pads are removed. The other extreme is when a poor-fitting saddle exerts such pressure that the blood supply in parts of the horse's back are restricting sweat production.

-Look for swelling on portions of the back, developing sores, or discoloration of the hair on the horse's back.

Some people have even suggested techniques as complicated as putting electronic pressure sensors on a horse's back under the saddle pads, or as simple as placing a clean white sheet under the pad and letting the sweat and dirt on the horse's back mark the pressure points.

Things to Check First

- Blankets and padding should be checked first if you think your horse has a sore back or suspect the saddle is not fitting properly. Worn or hard spots caused by sweat and dirt on the saddle pads can often cause problems. These spots should be brushed and washed out frequently.

- Is your under padding synthetic? Synthetic materials often do not let the horse's sweat evaporate or the back to breathe. Many just plain irritate a horse's back. You should always use a cotton, Mohair, or wool pad underneath the main pad to absorb the horse's sweat (much like a man's tee shirt.) Also, these are easier to wash and keep clean. Be sure to get all the detergent out after washing because that too can become an irritant.

- Are you using enough padding? Extra or better saddle pads can help a saddle fit more comfortable. However, do not pad so much that the saddle turns or rolls to the side. There are many emerging developments in the pad industry and you would be wise to keep up on this technology.

- Check for nails protruding from the saddle's fleece or sheep skin. It is surprising how often nails work loose under a saddle.

- Is your horse in shape? Is the horse overweight? Do you have a conditioning routine over several weeks to get your horse in shape before that long ride? During a conditioning period, their muscles develop and the skin toughens. An animal's body shape changes from season to season, and even during a day's riding. Weight gain or loss may change the saddle position and fit. Older animals tend to lose weight and have less muscle tone with more protruding bone structures.

Chapter Two - Overview of Saddles

To fit a saddle properly, we need a little background on the saddles themselves, their parts and pieces, the "trees" or understructure, and rigging types and positions.

Parts and Pieces

The western saddle has evolved through trial, error, and functional needs. The leather covering including the seat, swells, cantle, skirts, and jockeys form the protective 'housing" over the inner tree, much like shingles covering the roof of a house.

Figure 1 PARTS OF A MODERN SADDLE

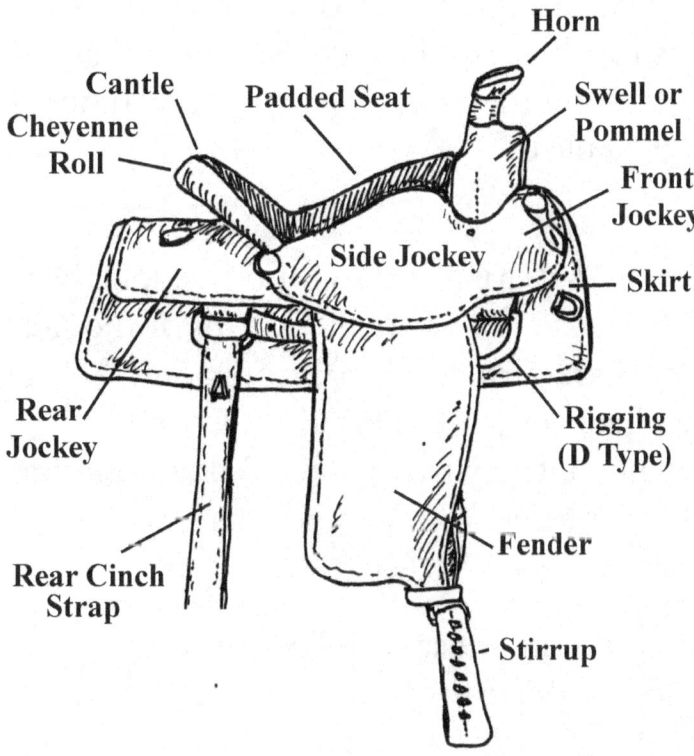

The Saddle Tree

The saddle tree forms the core of the saddle giving it shape, form, functionality, and strength. The primary job of the saddle tree is to distribute the rider's weight over the horse's back. There are scores and scores of different types of saddle trees based on history and needs. Some of the more prominent saddle-tree types include the Wade, several roper types, the Association, several barrel racing types, and reining and cutting styles. Other newer and less known are flex Tree, Treeless, Arabian, Gaited, Mule, Australian, and even Trophy. The other parts of a saddle including the bars, cantle, horn, etc., can also vary by type.

When you hear names such as Wade, or Bowman or Association, know that each of these names only identifies the tree as having a particular style of fork, horn, and cantle. Generally, the bars, gullet width and other certain factors in how a saddle fits a horse do not vary by type.

A tree consists of five basic parts – two bars that run parallel, the fork that holds the bars together at the front, the cantle that holds the bars together in the back, and the horn. The cutout or tunnel underneath the fork is called the gullet.

The bars are the weight-bearing surface of the saddle. Bars are made to contact the horses back to distribute the weight of the saddle and rider. Well–fitting bars of a western saddle will apply only ¾ lbs per square inch to the horse's back with a 150 lb rider. The entire length of the bars must be in even contact with the horse's back and the channel between the bars must be wide enough to keep pressure off the spine.

The gullet height and width must be sufficient to keep pressure off the withers and shoulders. Refer to Figure 2.

Figure 2 - The Saddle Tree

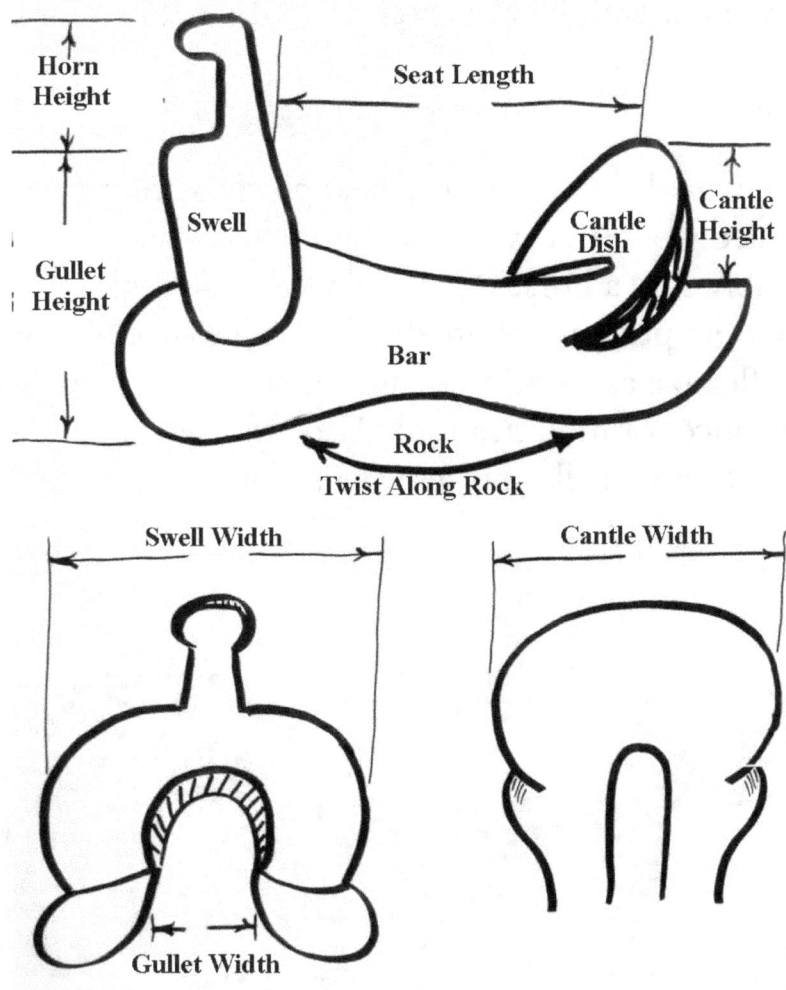

Important features to remember:

1. Rock is the curve along the bottom of the bars from front to back, much like a rocking chair.

2. Twist is the spline along the rock from front to back.

3. Flare is the curve at the front and back edges of the bars.

Saddle trees are traditionally made of wood, which is how they came to be called "trees". Usually softer woods are chosen for their flexibility – Ponderosa Pine, Beachwood, Ash, Cottonwood, Douglas fir. Once a tree is assembled, a covering is stretched over the tree for further strength. Rawhide is the traditional material, with lesser-quality trees covered with canvas, cheesecloth, goat skin, or fiberglass cloth. Trees are now even being built with Kevlar (bullet proof) coatings for extra strength.

After covering, a final coat of varnish is applied to seal the covering. An improperly-sealed wood tree will absorb moisture causing the tree to warp and possibly sore a horse. Synthetic trees are built of plastic or fiberglass in a mold process. Synthetic trees have several limitations. They aren't as flexible as wood trees and since they're made with molds, there is little chance for modification. Also, synthetic materials do not seem to be able to hold nails and screws used in assembly as well as wooden trees. See Figure 3.

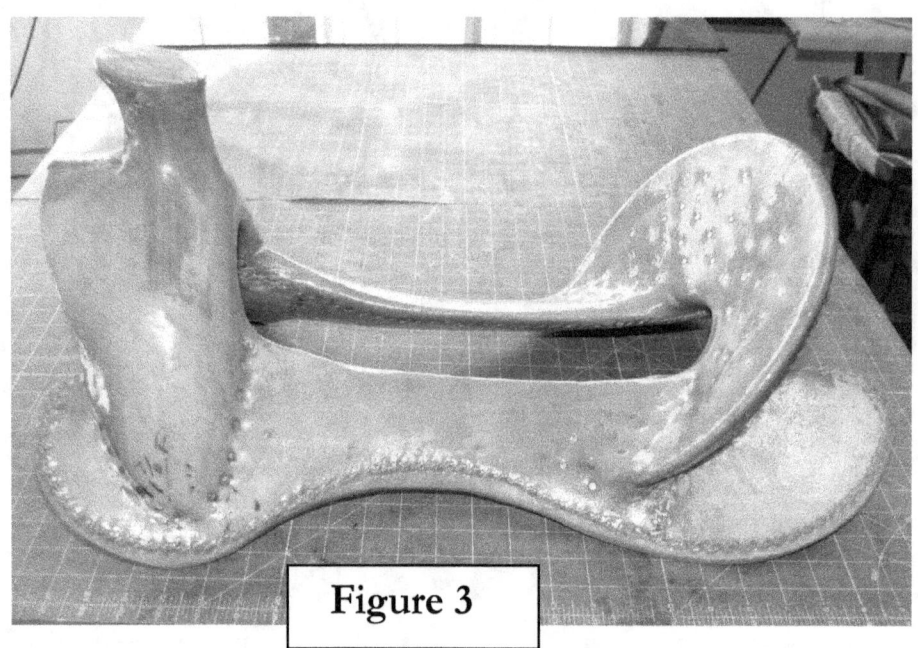

Figure 3

A modern saddle tree built of pine and covered with rawhide.

There are not any specific industry standards for saddle tree measurements. Different tree makers measure trees differently and even call the same trees by different names.

The Seat

Seat size usually refers to rider fit but can also have an impact on how the saddle fits the horse. As a general rule, there should be about four inches between the front of your body and the fork or swells of the saddle. Some of the published guidelines for seat size are:

Youth:	12 to 13 inches
Small Adult:	14 inches
Average Adult:	15 inches
Large Adult:	16 inches
Extra large adult:	17 inches

However, be aware there is no industry standard for seat length other than the measurement from the back of the fork to the top of the cantle. There are a number of variables to consider in measuring seat length because different tree styles (Wade, roper, pleasure, etc.) are all different. These include seat depth, seat or cantle slope, cantle dish, fork style and fork angle. Refer to Figure 4.

Because of cantle angle, cantle height, fork height, and fork angle, the measurement of seat length is not standard between styles of trees.

Seat length can have a direct effect on how a saddle fits a horse. The bars on the saddle can only extend behind the cantle approximately 4 inches So when seat length changes, the bars change in length. This results in less bar surface on the horse's back with a shorter seat versus extending the bars on a longer seat length such as in a 17-inch saddle. With a short-back horse, a 17-inch seat could place the rear of the bars directly over the horse's kidneys. See Figures 5 and 6.

Figure 4 - Seat Length Varies by Style

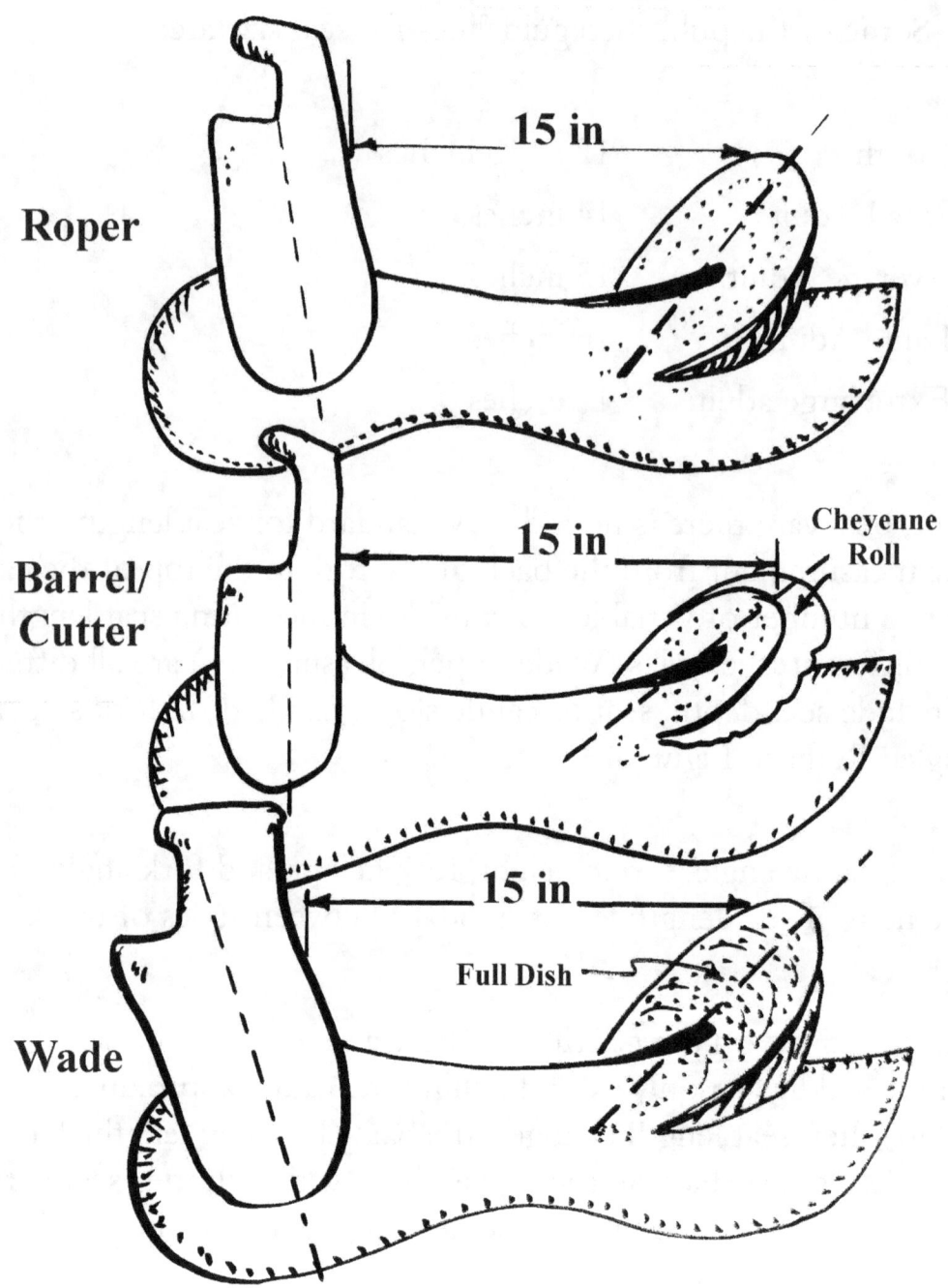

Figure 5 - Seat Length Affects Bar Length

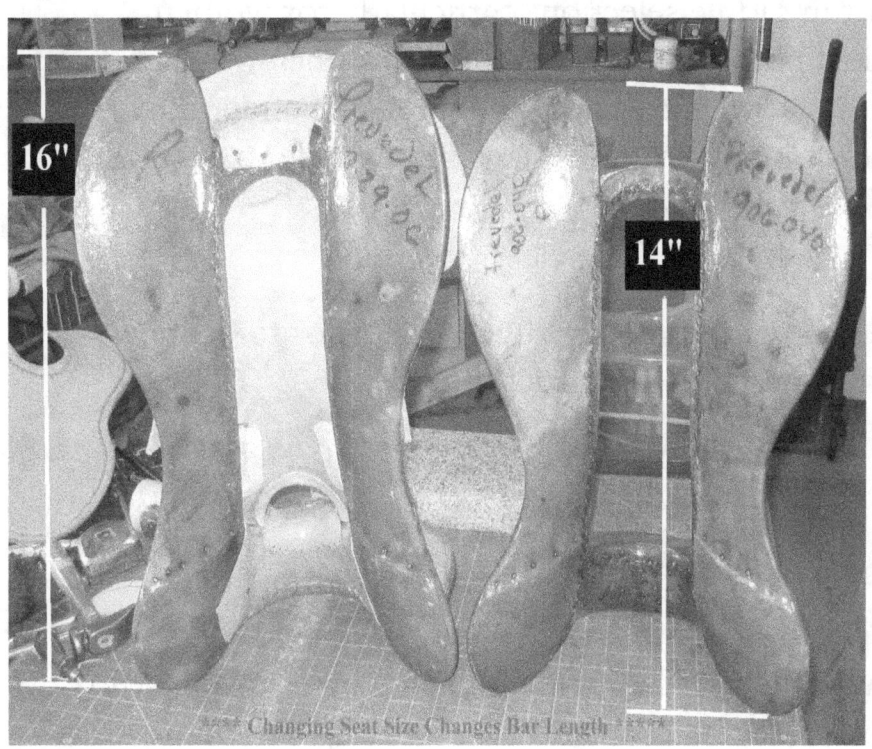

Figure 5 shown at the left illustrates a comparison of a 16-inch-seat saddle tree and a 14-inch-seat saddle tree. Note the difference in bar length and bar area with the trees.

Rider weight is the main concern when selecting a smaller seat size.

Figure 6 - The Effect of Different Seat Lengths

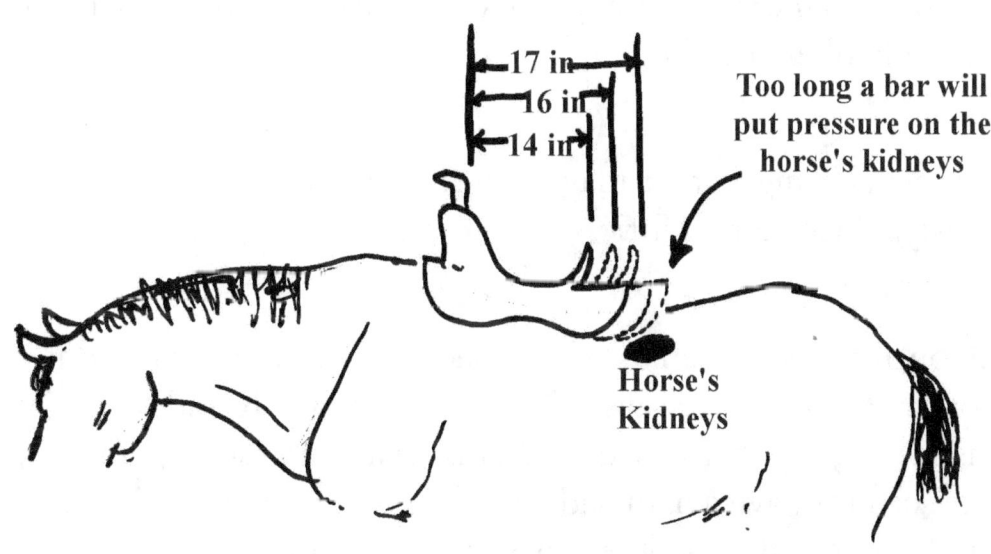

Too long a bar will put pressure on the horse's kidneys

Horse's Kidneys

Saddle Weight

Saddle weight is a factor in saddle selection, particularly for women. Manufacturers have taken note of this and are now producing a variety of lighter-weight saddles. However, "under the hood" or under the saddle leather, several major compromises have to be made to achieve this lighter weight.

- The quality of the tree may be sacrificed. Composite fiberglass or poly-resin may be used to construct the tree.

- The rawhide covering may be replaced with varnish, fiberglass cloth, thinner rawhide such as goat skin, etc.

- The leather under the bars is often eliminated and replaced with a thin stiff masonite material. In addition to being like riding on a board, the shearling lining will not adhere to this material with glue so pneumatic nails are applied into the bars to hold all the materials in place. It is not uncommon to find 20 to 30 nails on each bar side.

- Sheep skin (shearling) linings may be replaced with artificial or man-made fiber shearling.

- Thinner skirting leather may be used or the skirting may be a nylon-type (Cordura) fabric.

Generally, construction materials relate specifically to how that saddle will fit a horse. An old adage says: "You can have a light saddle that is poorly constructed, or a heavy saddle that is well constructed, but generally you cannot have a light saddle that is well constructed"......... Remember - A good fitting saddle starts with a quality tree!

Gullet Width

The gullet of a saddle can come in several sizes much like a man's tee shirt (small, medium, and large). Keep in mind that there is no industry standard for this measurement, nor is there even common agreement where the gullet should be measured. Almost all literature refers to gullet width as the key to saddle fitting, however, it is just one of several variables to be considered. Since there is just 1/4 inch between sizes, its importance is diminished when considering the total distance between the horse's withers, the effect of padding, and rigging position. Reference Figure 7.

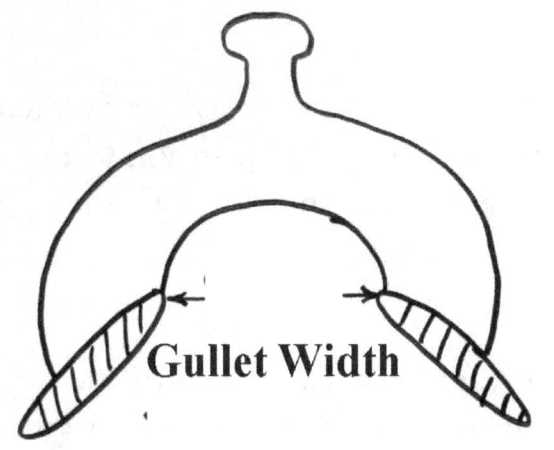

Figure 7 - Gullet Width

Semi-quarter horse gullet width:	6 ¼ inches
Regular quarter horse gullet width:	6 ½ inches
Full quarter horse gullet width:	6 ¾ inches
Arabian Bars:	6 ¼ to 6 ¾ with a flatter pitch

Eighty to ninety percent of today's horses have conformation that will be comfortable in either a standard semi-quarter horse or quarter horse tree. The larger full quarter horse trees generally have bars flared out to accommodate a wider animal, such as those with a "mutton back" conformation.

The Saddle Rigging

Saddle rigging is one of the key points in fitting a saddle to the horse's back. It is probably the most misunderstood functionality of any saddle part. Rigging position determines where the cinch goes around the horse's girth. The names of the different front rig positions are derived from their distance from the cantle to the fork.

Most important is the knowledge that riggings can be adjusted or even replaced. Riggings are categorized as either single or double. Double riggings have additional D rings or slots for attaching a back cinch. Today, most saddles are double rigged.

It is important to note, that the standard D or ring hanging from below the cantle can only be used in the full position, other wise, the stirrup leathers would be restricted in swinging forward. To compensate for this, the Stohlman style, a modified-standard style, was developed.

There is no distinct advantage between any of the rigging types. Equestrian people will continue to debate, for instance, if an in-skirt rigging is any stronger than a conventional standard D or ring-type rig. As a rule, roping and cutting saddles do not come with in-skirt riggings. On the other hand, most barrel, reiner, show and pleasure saddles have in-skirt rigs. This is probably more a result of tradition rather than any particular advantage. A flat plate "hanging rigging" is sort of in between. Refer to Figure 8.

Historically, early saddles before the western saddle did not have fixed riggings. This allowed for the moving of the rigging as various saddles were used with different horses. See Figure 9.

Figure 8 — COMMON TYPES OF RIGGINGS

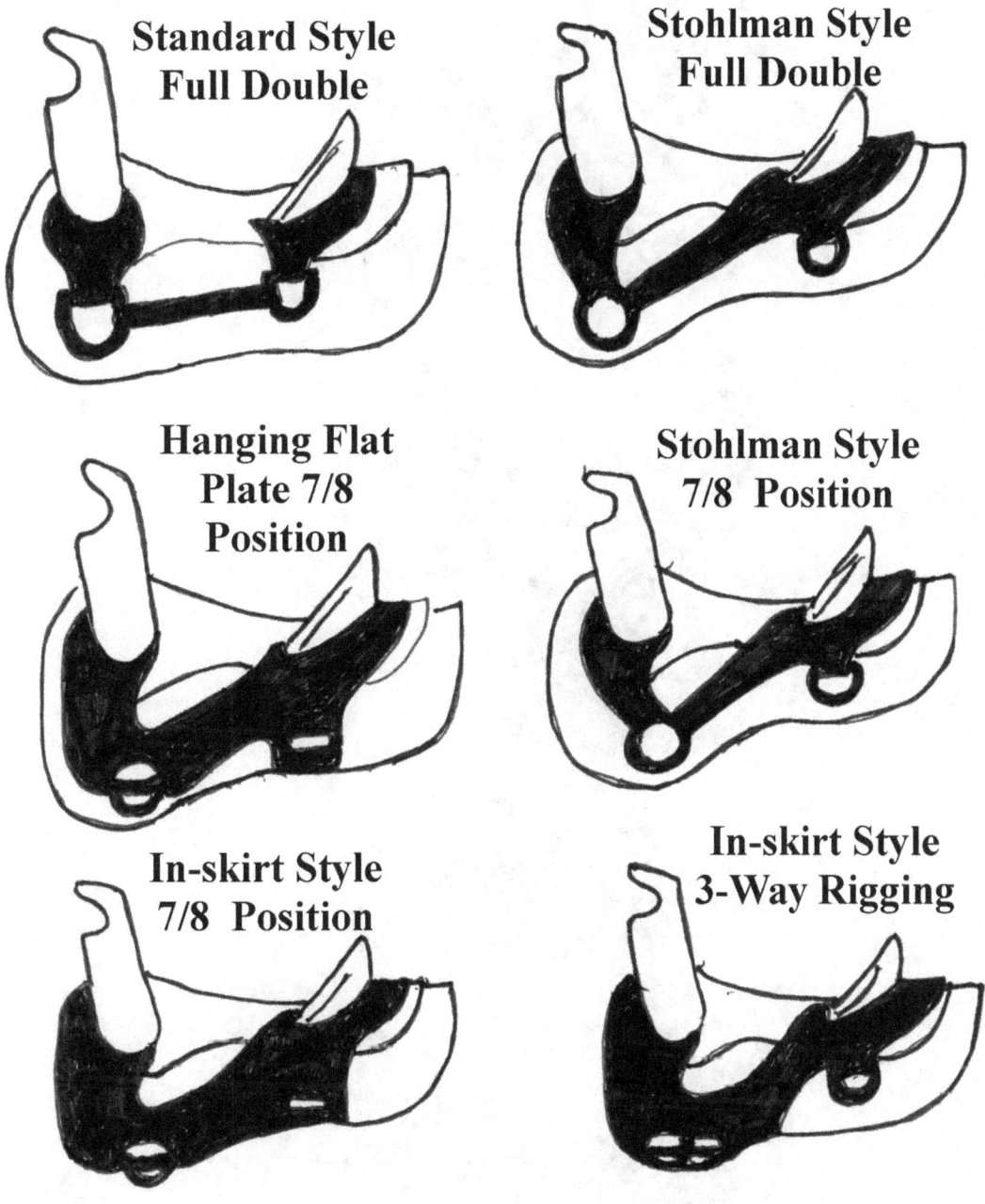

Figure 9 - Historic Riggings

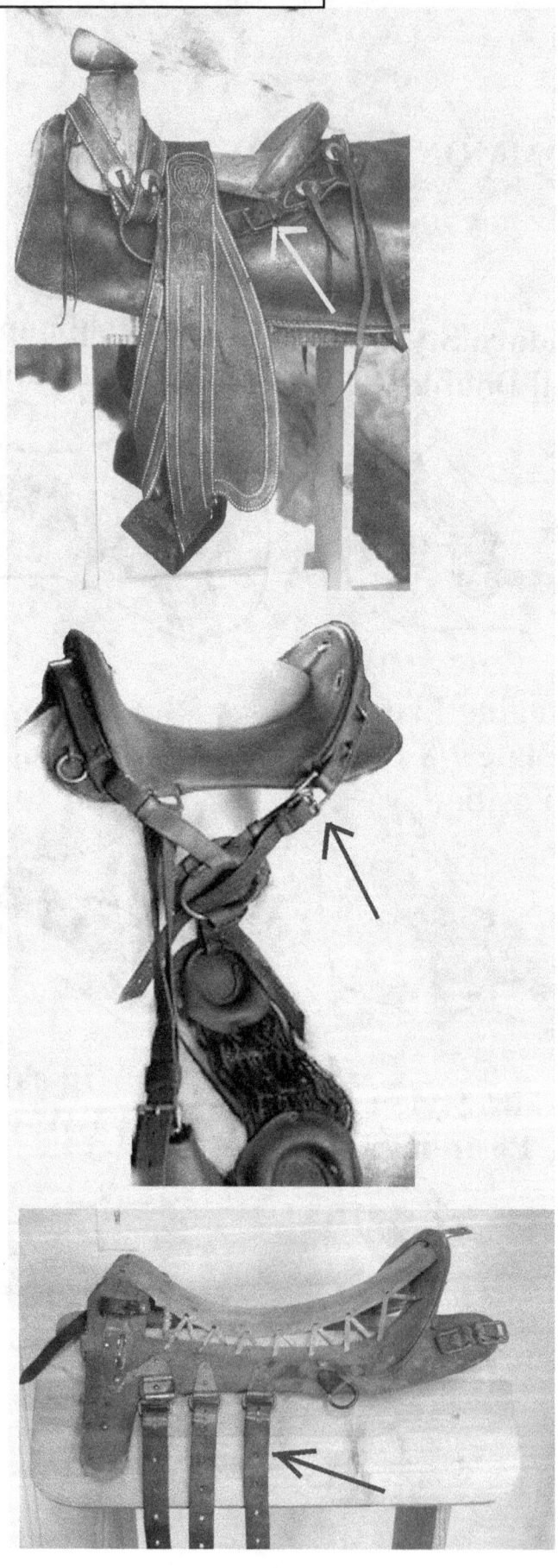

Figure 9 Discussion

Where did we go wrong? The concept of adjustable rigging position goes back hundreds of years. To the left are three examples of historic rigging positions.

The top saddle is a Mexican saddle from the late 1800s. Note the buckle on the rear cinch-ring strap (white arrow) allows the rigging to be adjusted forward or back.

The middle saddle is a US Calvary saddle (Model 1904) which has the same adjustable tie strap to the cinch ring.

The bottom saddle is a World War II German Calvary saddle with three cinch straps that tie to a two buckle surcingle cinch. This also allows the positioning of the saddle forward or back upon the horse.

Sometime after the Civil War, western saddle makers dropped adjustable riggings and started making saddles with fixed, non-adjustable riggings. This modification got away from straps as cinch-ring supports in favor of thicker and wider leather attachments that would hold up on the long trail drives. It was a long walk home if a strap broke. The large skirts covering these early saddles also contributed to this design change.

Rigging Positions

Rigging position is where the cinch strap hooks onto the saddle to hold it in place. The girth or cinch strap position on a horse is a physical given. How many times have you put your saddle in a more forward place on your horse, only to have the cinch work back to the same girth position? Therefore, the rigging position is used to position the saddle over the girth.

There are four rigging positions that have been traditionally used on western saddles.

These are full, seven-eighths, three-quarter, and center fire. In theory, the center of gravity for a horse is near the top of the shoulders or the seven-eighths position. Seven-eighths rigs are the most popular for pleasure riding. Full-position rigs are mostly used on roping saddles to keep the saddle behind the center of gravity. This allows the horse to more efficiently pull a dallied or tight rope. Most full and seven-eighths riggings require a back cinch to keep the saddle from tipping forward. Note the full position is directly under the center of the fork.

The center position (center fire) rigs were mostly used 100 years ago to break and ride the mustang-type horses of the day. Today, center positions are mostly used on endurance saddles. See Figures 10 and 11.

Figure 10 - Rigging Positions

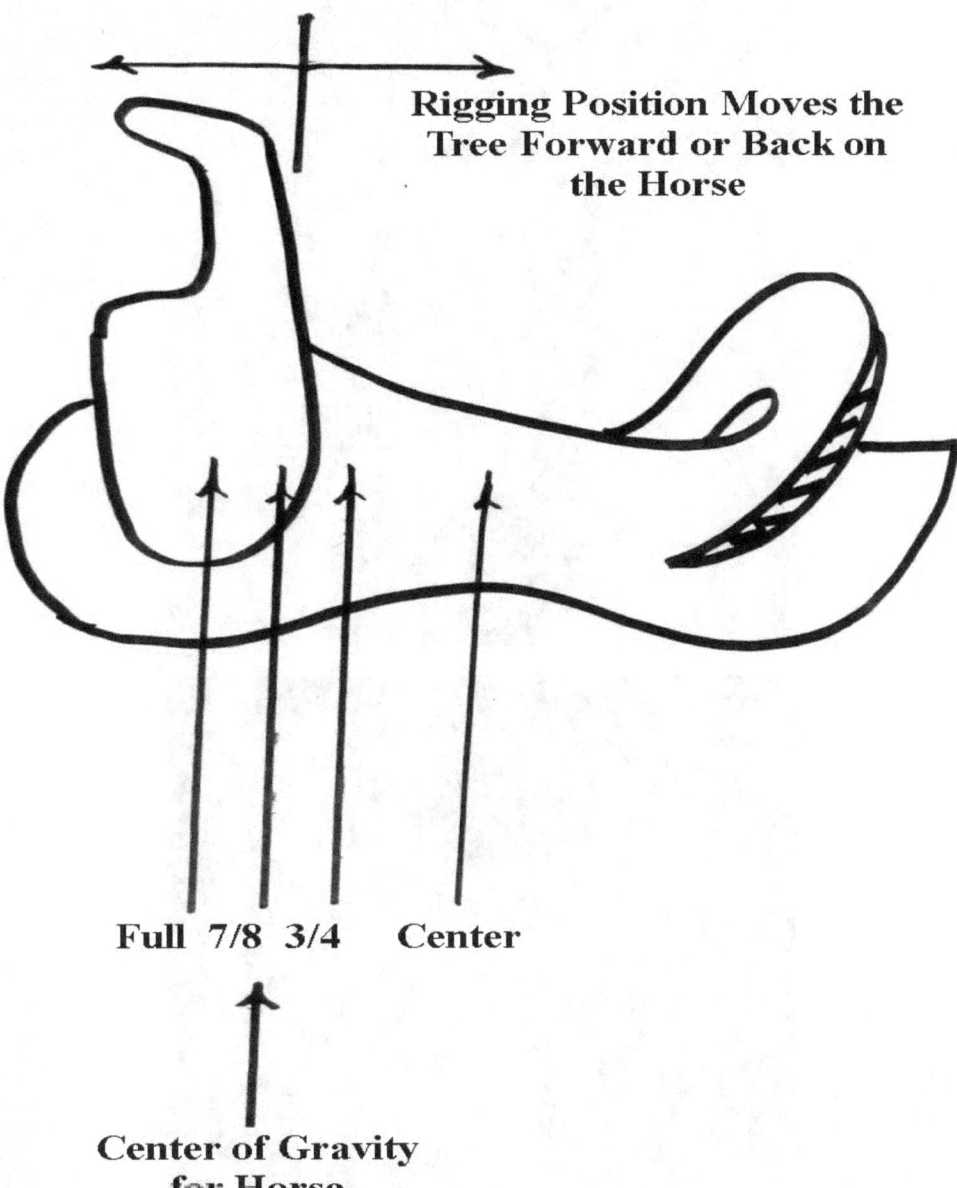

Figure 11 - Illustrations of Rigging Position

Figure 11 Discussion

Left top - A full position rigged saddle - This is a Bowman roper style. Note that the standard rigging D lines up directly with a perpendicular line through the center of the pommel or fork (white line).

This rigging position is made to hold the saddle behind the horse's shoulders and behind the center of gravity.

Left bottom - This is a seven-eighths rigged saddle in a Wade hanging plate style. Here the hanging plate single D lines up behind the center of the fork or swell (white line).

This rigging positions the saddle more over the shoulders and upon the center of gravity of the horse.

Note that the annotations of "over the center of gravity" and "behind the center of gravity" do not signify that the saddles will fit a horse properly. It only expresses the position that the saddle is held on the horse.

Chapter 3 - Saddle Fitting Guide

We all know horses have different shaped backs, high and low withers, different back lengths, and may or may not have prominent shoulder bones. Several things need to be checked to see if a saddle is fitted or positioned properly. Be sure the horse's head is up while checking.

Step One - Check Gullet Height and Width

These two measurements are interrelated. Many old saddles produced before the 1940s were designed with very narrow gullets (less than 5 1/2 inches) to fit the mustang-type horses of the day. It is almost impossible to make one of these saddles fit on a modern horse. Also be aware, that during the late 1940s and 1950s, the roper-dogger type saddles were built with very low gullet heights as a style to fit rodeo performers. These saddles have caused a lot of nasty sores and galls on the top of the withers of many horses. See Figure 12.

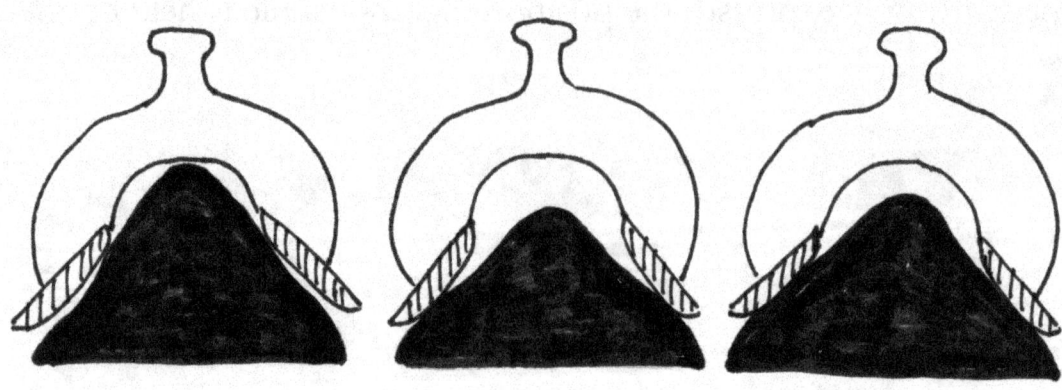

Figure 12 - Examples of Different Gullet Widths

Gullet Too Wide - Sores on Top of Withers

Gullet Too Narrow - Pinches Withers

Correct Fit !!!

In Summary,
- If the saddle is too narrow, there will tend to be contact at the bottom of the bar and not at the top
- If the saddle is too wide, there could be contact with the withers at the top of the gullet. Also, only the top of the bar(s) may be in contact with the horse's back.
- The main point to check is the clearance at the withers. Use the 2 to 4 finger rule. See Figure 13.
- Note: Problems with gullet width and height can also be caused by rigging position. A tree in the full position and quarter-horse gullet width (6 1/2 inches) could rub on the withers. When moved to the 7/8 rigging position, clearance on the withers could be fine. The question then remains, if the rigging is moved to the 7/8, will the bars impact the shoulder blades while the horse is running, or will a bridge develop between the horse's back and the bars? Refer to Figure 13.

Step Two - Check the Bar Flare

The corners of the bars or bar flare should be checked on both front and back of the tree. The ends should not be digging into the horse, but should have a slight flare where some space exists. Insufficient bar flare on the front can restrict the horse's movement, and not enough flare on the rear, particularly if the rider is heavy, can cause sores. Short-backed and/or sway-backed horses seem more susceptible to this. If this occurs, it is a technical fix to modify or repair the tree. See Figure 14.

Figure 13 - Gullet Examples

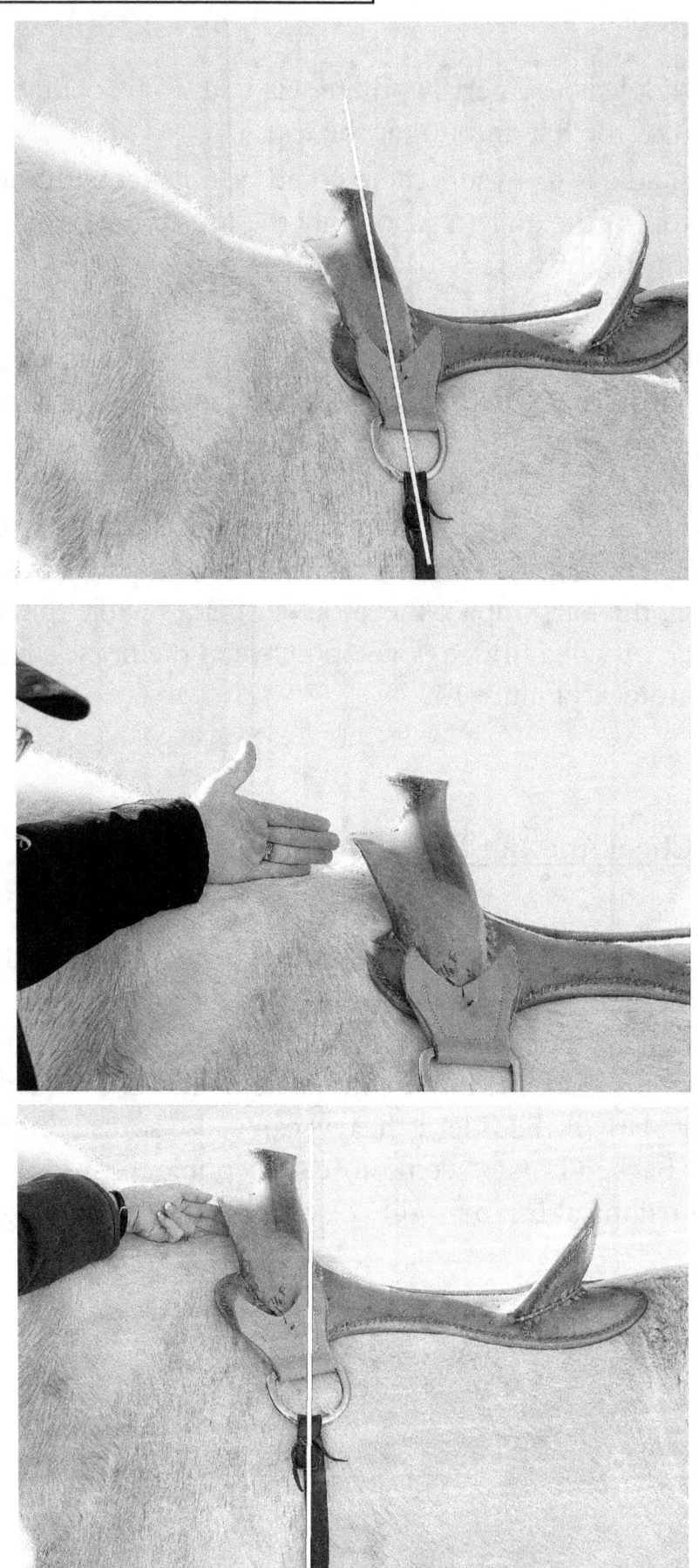

Figure 13 Discussion

Top Left - Example of a saddle rigged in the full position on a narrow-withered horse. The gullet is too wide in this position and the girth line is at an angle because the front of the saddle is so low. Also notice that the rear of the saddle sticks up. This saddle tree has a quarter horse gullet spacing of 6 1/2 inches. By resting on the top of the horse's withers, the gullet would quickly sore this horse.

Left Center - With the gullet resting so low on the withers, no fingers can be inserted under the gullet. As a rule, there should be room for two to four stacked fingers in the space.

Left Bottom - However, when the rigging is changed to the 7/8 position (white line) and the saddle tree moved forward, there is now space for at least two fingers under the gullet. Note that on this particular horse, in the 7/8 position, the rock of the bars fit snugly on the horse's back.

However, keep in mind that on many horses, this change to a 7/8 position could cause bridging and the remedies would be to (1) change to a semi-quarter tree in full position, or (2) build up the rock for a 7/8 position.

Step Three - Check Clearance on Shoulders

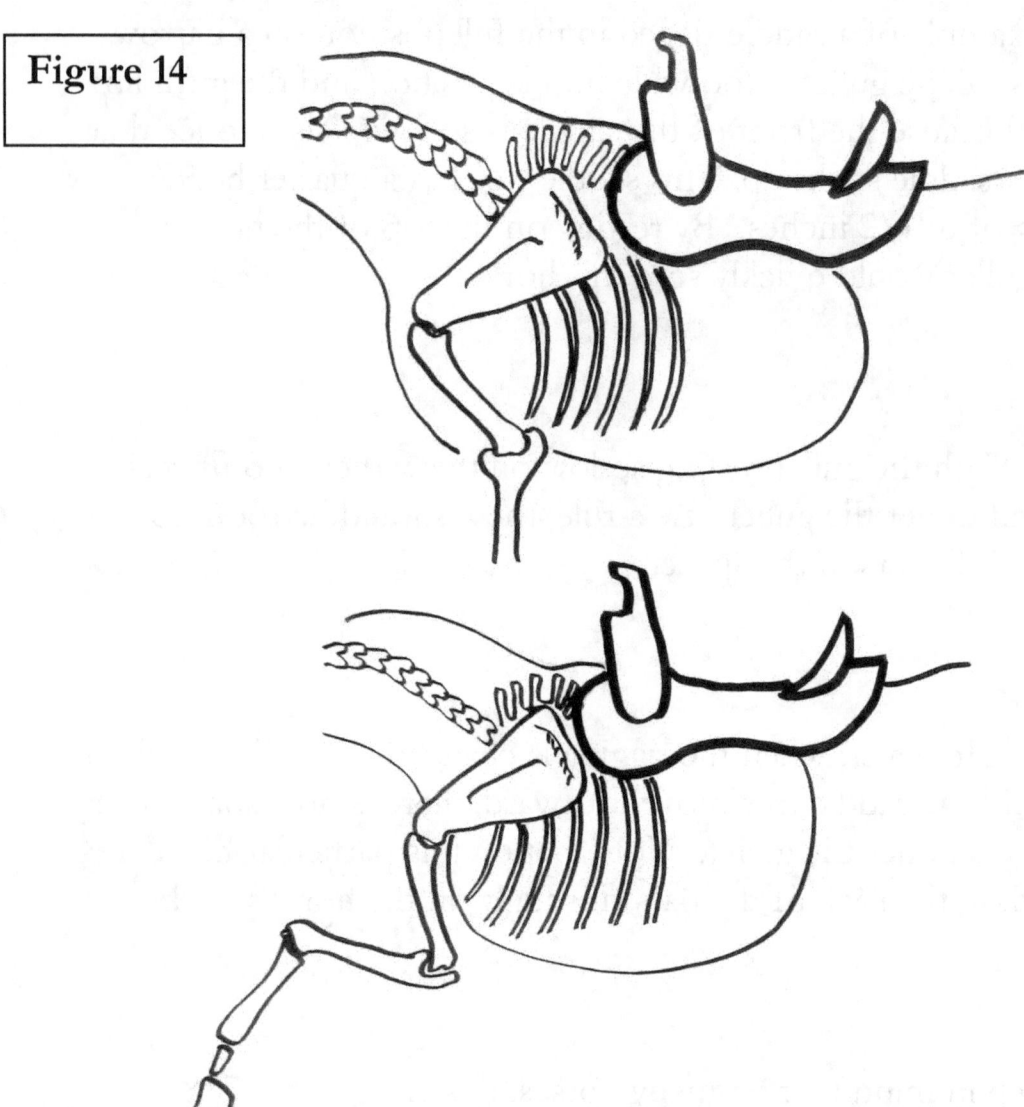

Figure 14

A saddle rigged to move the saddle forward may strike the horse's shoulder blade while running. This is a concern with large-boned horses with high shoulder blades.

Step Four - Check Rigging Position

Here, there are three areas of concern:

    1. Bridging: - contact on the front (withers) and rear (croup) of the horse's back by the bars, but not in the center. You can usually tell bridging is occurring if there are sores or white hairs in the withers and/or croup area, the horse's back is tender to touch, or the horse acts up, tosses its head, or even becomes unmanageable. Sweat spots on the horse's back or saddle pads- blanket after riding may also be evident. Much like a highway bridge, the bars of a saddle can bridge the horse's back and the contact points or abutments, sore the horse. The length of a horse's back, particularly long-backed breeds, can also cause bridging. Refer to Figure 15.

Figure 15 - Example of Bridging of the Bars

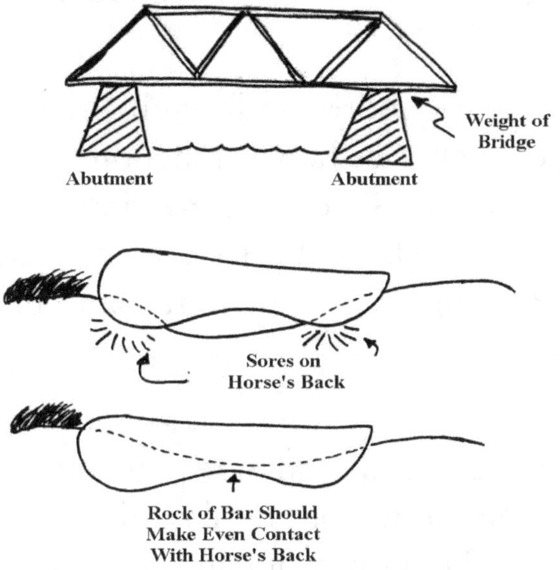

- Weight of Bridge
- Abutment
- Abutment
- Sores on Horse's Back
- Rock of Bar Should Make Even Contact With Horse's Back

The solutions to bridging include adding more padding, moving the rigging position, and building up the rock of the bars.

2. Not Enough Rock – Compounding bridging, insufficient rock occurs when there is insufficient bend in the bars to fit the horse's back. It is mainly confined to horses with sway backs, deformities, or very high withers, but can also occur in larger-boned horses.

3. Too Much Rock - This is when there is too much bend in the bar. It makes the saddle contact in the middle of the back and less in the front and back. The saddle may pitch forward when cinched up and the rear of the saddle may stick up. Don't confuse this with too wide of a gullet.

Methods for Checking on Bridging and Rock

Determining bridging and rock problems are more difficult tasks of saddle fitting. Because of the fleece, skirts, and jockeys, you cannot see if the bars of a saddle are making contact with the horse.

First, determine the rigging position of your saddle based on the criteria in Chapter Two. Then try to determine, based on your horse's back, what its physical rigging position should be. Here are **three separate** suggestions on how to do this:

- Borrow a neighbor's saddle with a rigging position different than yours and see how it functions on your horse. Even better is to try a saddle that has an existing three-way rigging (more about this later). This may not be an exact measurement, but if it answers your question, you have succeeded.

- Use an uncovered saddle tree on your horse. See if you can borrow one from your local saddle maker or a friend. Basic wood trees without any covering such as rawhide, can be purchased from tree manufacturers for a reduced charge, or you can even purchase one cheaply on E-Bay. Remember there are no industry standards on trees, but assume you can acquire one that is close enough in length, rock, and twist to work.

As a last resort, remove the skirting from your saddle to see how the bars contact the back of your horse (Generally this is not as difficult as it sounds). Instructions for saddle disassembly are in the appendix.

Once the tree is on the horse's back, check the rigging position to see if it is properly positioned to hold the saddle where it should be. The proper position should have no gaps and the bars should make contact along the entire bar length. If the proper position is different than the rigging position on your existing saddle, then use instructions in Chapter 4 on how to modify your saddle. From this you can determine if a horse is better fit with a full or 7/8 rigging using a standard saddle tree. If there are still gaps, but the tree seems to fit better in the new position, you may have to build up the rock of the bars. Instructions are in Chapter 4. Refer to Figures 16 and 17.

Figure 16

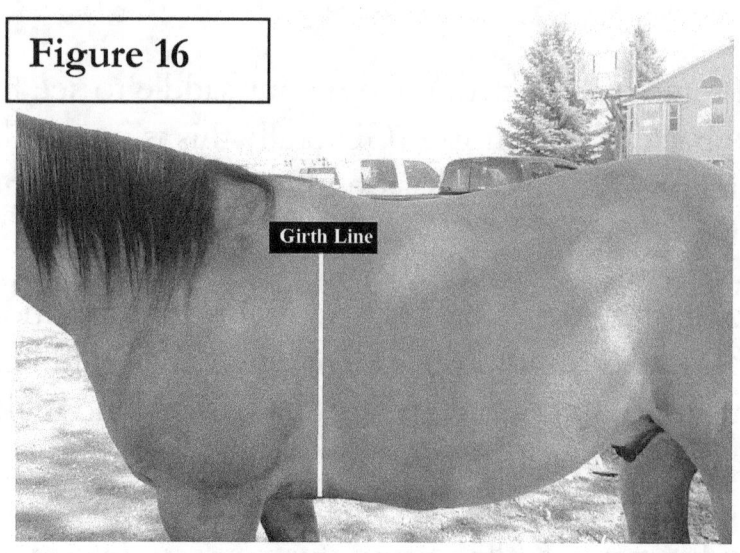

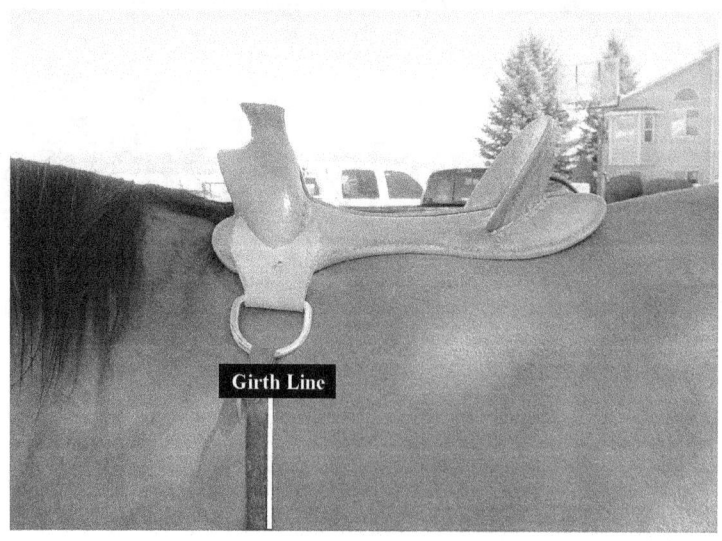

Figure 16 Discussion

Left Top - Pictured is a low-withered horse with the cinch or girth line marked in white. A saddle holding the cinch in this position can be assumed to fit correctly. But what is the rigging position?

Left Middle - A tree on this horse with the rigging in the 7/8 position. Note the gap under the bars as shown by the leather insert. The bars are definitely not making contact with the back. This is an example of bridging. Sores would develop on this horse's back where the bars are making contact.

Left bottom - The tree has been moved to the full position. Note the rigging lines up with the girth line and there are no gaps or spaces under the bars. Good contact is being made the entire length of the bars. This horse requires a rigging in the full position.

Figure 17

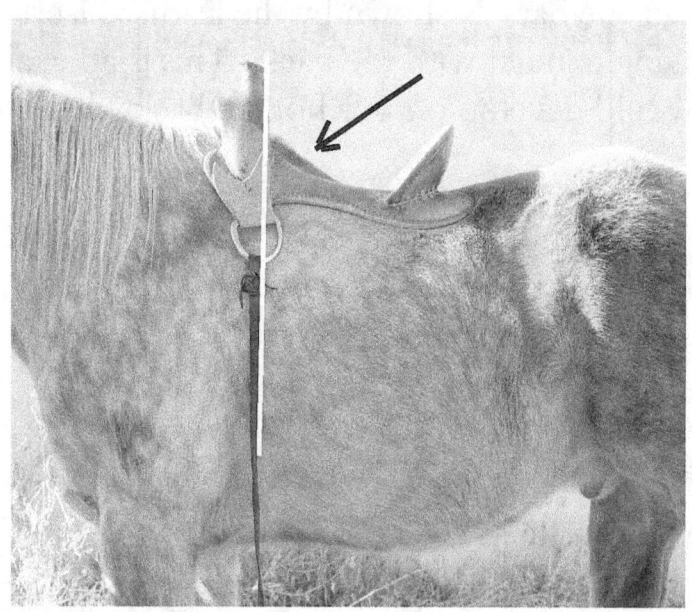

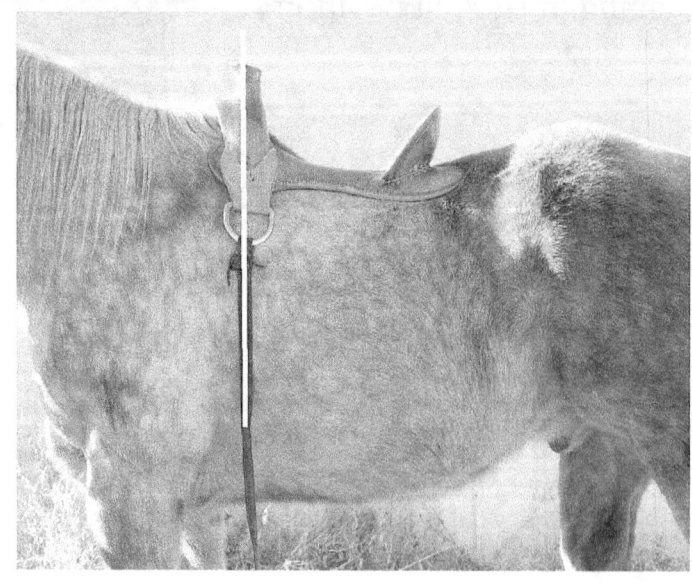

Figure 17 Discussion

Left Top - This horse has fairly dominant withers. When ridden, the saddle on this horse tends to slip back and a breast collar is required to hold the 7/8 rigging saddle in place. This horse has a typical quarter horse conformation. Note the large shoulder blades leading up to the withers.

Left Center - When the tree in 7/8 position was placed on the horse, the bars fit well as did the gullet height. However, notice the amount of backbone exposed up through the center of the tree. This is pushing against the seat of the saddle, forcing the saddle to slide back. Also note how the saddle tree bars are held up on the prominent shoulder blades of the horse and how the rear of the bars are digging into the horse's back.

Left Bottom - In the full position, the tree is behind the shoulder blades and less backbone is exposed. This is a much more comfortable position for this horse.

Chapter 4 - Solutions to Saddle-Fitting Problems

After you have evaluated the "Things to Check First" in Chapter One and you and your horse still have problems, then some modification of your saddle may be in order. Using the knowledge you gained in Chapter 3, you should have some idea if the rigging position or rock of the bars, or both, need to be changed.

This chapter discusses (1) rigging position adjustments that are fairly minor and someone with high school shop aptitude or experience with carpentry can accomplish this, and (2) changing the rock of the bars which is a little more technical, but do-able with a few shop tools. However, as a rule of caution, DO NOT TRY ANY OF THESE FIRST ON YOUR WIFE'S SADDLE!

Some tools you will need to complete all the modifications include a large Phillips screw driver, hammer, electric drill, leather glue, copper leather rivets (one inch #9s), a rivet setter, side cutter pliers, a skiving knife, and #10 wood screws. Some small pieces of saddle leather (13-15 pound weight) may also be needed. Generally, small pieces of scrap leather can be purchased from feed or tack stores or other leather suppliers. Patterns for the Standard Rigging leathers are included in the Appendix. Make sure that none of the leather used is from the "belly" area. A good test is to wet the leather for a few seconds and then pull on it. If it's belly, it will stretch. A leather needle and some waxed thread are optional materials.

The Three-way Rigging

The three-way rigging is probably the easiest and most efficient way to change rigging positions on a saddle. Saddles with this built-in feature can be used on many different horses with varying backs. By using a three-way, saddles can be placed in the full, 7/8 or 3/4 position at the rider's option. It is also a great way to find which rigging position is most comfortable to your horse.

Figure 18 is an example of how to use a three-way with latigos. Note that latigos must be used on both sides of the saddle if the 7/8 configuration is to be used. A billet on the off side of the saddle must be replaced with a latigo. In the 7/8 position, latigo tie-off knots are always tied on the forward ring so no lump forms under the rider's leg.

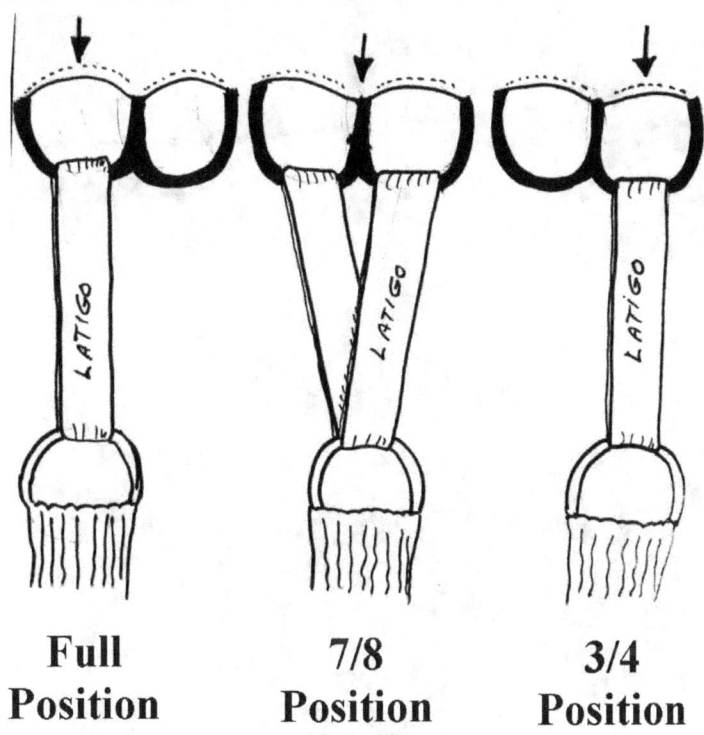

Figure 18 - How to Use a Three Way Rigging

Full Position   **7/8 Position**   **3/4 Position**

Figure 19 - Examples of Three Way Riggings

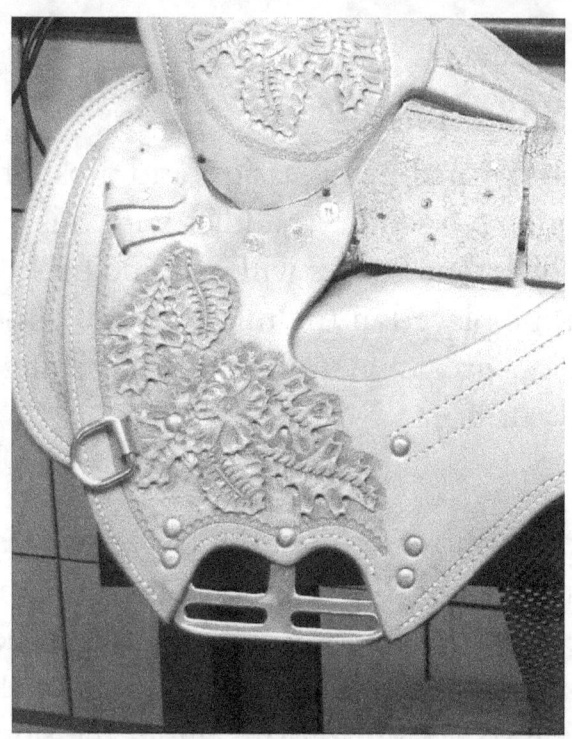

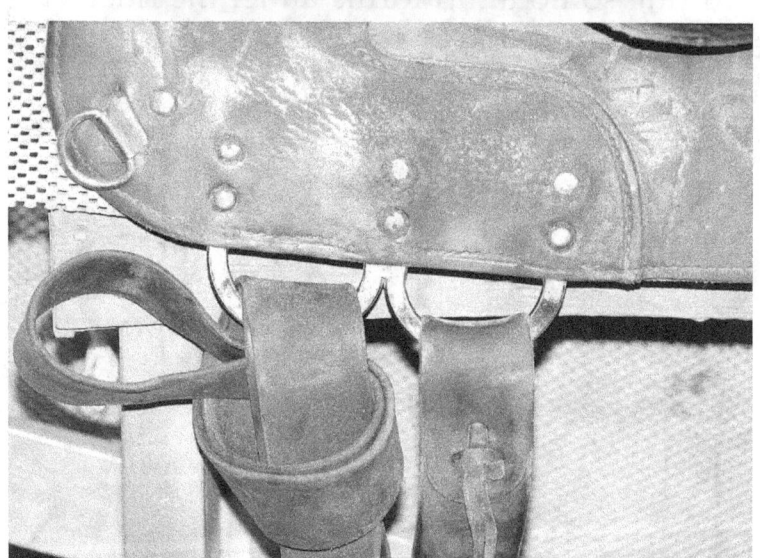

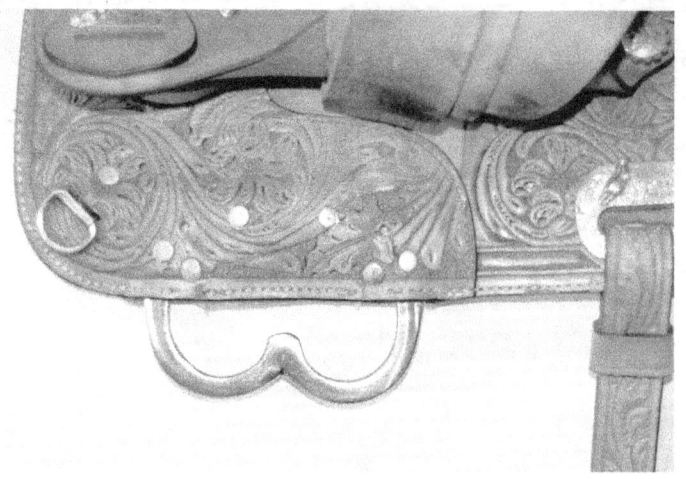

Figure 19 Discussion

Left Top - Example of a brass three-way rigging in hanging-plate configuration on a Wade tree. Locations of places to purchase three-way riggings are included in the Appendix.

Left Middle - A conventional nickel-plated three-way rig riveted into the skirt of a saddle.

Never pass up an option to purchase a saddle with this type of rigging. How to install three-way rigging is also included later in this section.

Left Bottom - This type of rigging is also available in a jump three-way option with a gap in the middle post allowing the rider to change the position by 'jumping' the billet and latigo without having to un-cinch the horse.

Modifying Rigging Positions

If you are unsure about proceeding with these instructions, seek professional help or guidance before you modify or cut into your saddles.

1. How To Do It

First, determine what type of rigging you currently have in your saddle. Refer to Figure 8 on page 15.

For most modifications of rigging position, the skirts of the saddle do not have to be removed. The jockeys and conchos will have to be removed to modify or add a hanging plate rig or a Standard or Stohlman type rigs.

You cannot modify a saddle that is not constructed as an in-skirt (i.e. one with an existing Standard D or ring rig) to a three way in-skirt rigging because there is no upper rigging leather sewn into the skirting that attaches to the bars just below the cantle swell. This in essence, doubles the leather for strength and allows the three way to be sandwiched or riveted between the two leathers.

In-skirt riggings can be converted to any of the Standard or Stohlman "D" type riggings. The only disadvantage is that the new rigging will be in a fixed position and not adjustable as with a three way.

Refer to Figure 20 for a Rigging Conversion Guide.

See Figures 21 thru 27 for examples.

Figure 20 - Rigging Conversion Guide

Existing Rigging for Conversion	Rigging Type Allowed
Standard "D" - Full Position	Stohlman 3/4, 7/8 Hanging Plate Single Hanging Plate Three Way
Stohlman 3/4, 7/8	Standard D Full Position Hanging Plate Single Hanging Plate Three Way
Hanging Plate Single 7/8	Hanging Plate Three Way Standard D Full Position Stohlman 3/4, 7/8
In-skirt Single 7/8	In-skirt Three Way Standard D Full Stohlman 3/4, 7/8 Hanging Plate Single Hanging Plate Three Way

2. Working Examples

Modifying the In-skirt 7/8 Rig to a Three-way In-skirt

Figure 21

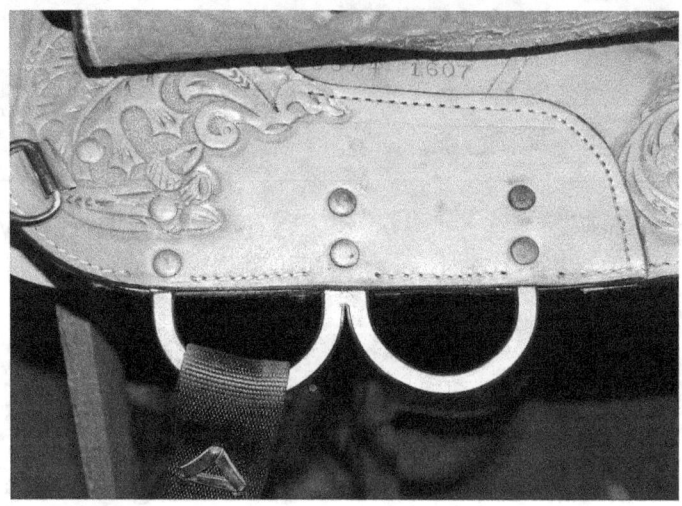

Figure 21 Discussion

Left Top - Example showing position of nickel plated three-way rig over in-skirt rigging in 7/8 position. This conversion is just a matter of peeling up the fleece on the back side, drilling out the existing rigging rivets, punching new holes to match the three-way hardware, sandwiching the new three-way rig into the skirt, inserting and capping copper rivets (#9 size) to hold the three-way rig in place, and then gluing down the fleece on the underside. Rivets can also be placed in the old holes for cosmetic purposes.

Left Bottom - The three-way rigging is a very adaptable and attractive type of rigging that lies flat and will hold any saddle in place. Saddles with this type of rigging can be used on many different horses by adjusting through which ring the latigo passes.

In-skirt 7/8 position to a Full Position Standard D

Figure 22

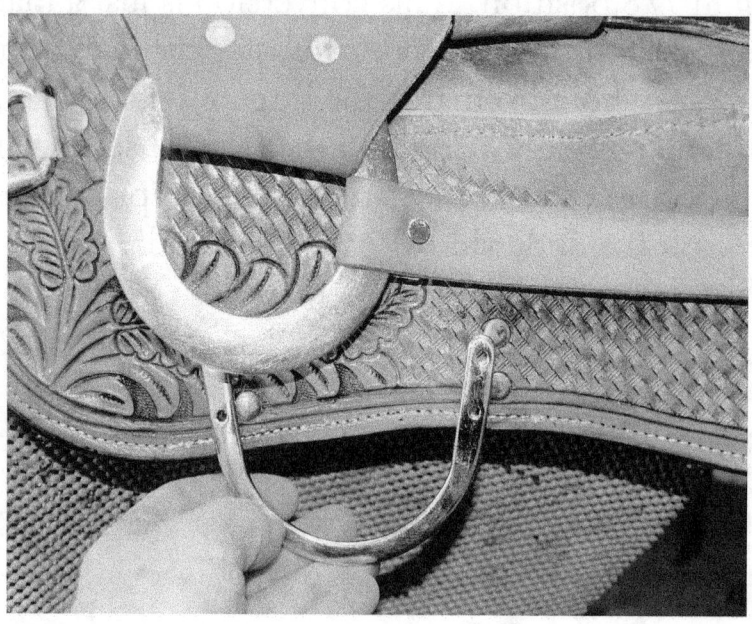

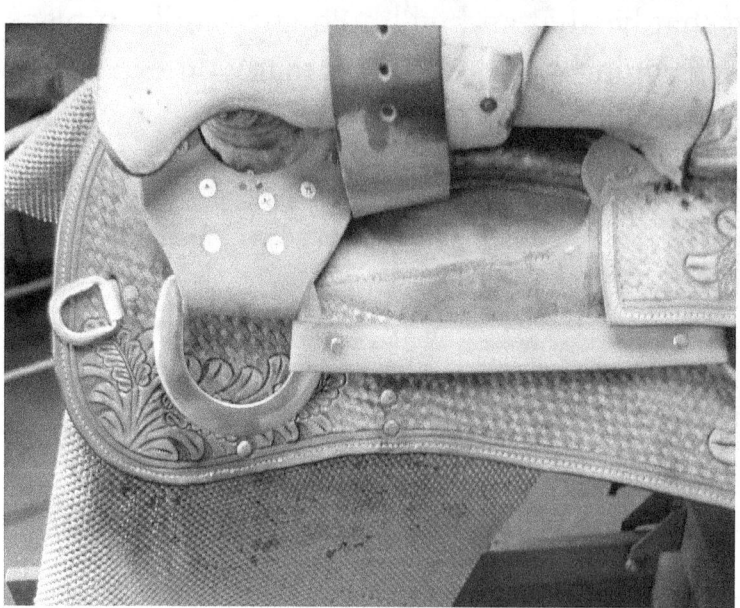

Figure 22 Discussion

Left Top - In this image, the 7/8 in-skirt rigging has been replaced with a Standard Double D rig in the full position. Notice how the old holes in the skirt have been filled in with rivets to maintain the aesthetics of the saddle. Patterns for front and back standard rigging leathers are included in the appendix.

Left Bottom - Wider view of the conversion. Note the hobble strap connecting the front D to the rear D. If the saddle lacked a rear D, the strap would tie to behind the seat or cantle. It is needed to prevent the front D from being pulled too far forward, allowing the saddle to slip back.

Single In-skirt Rig to a Stohlman Standard

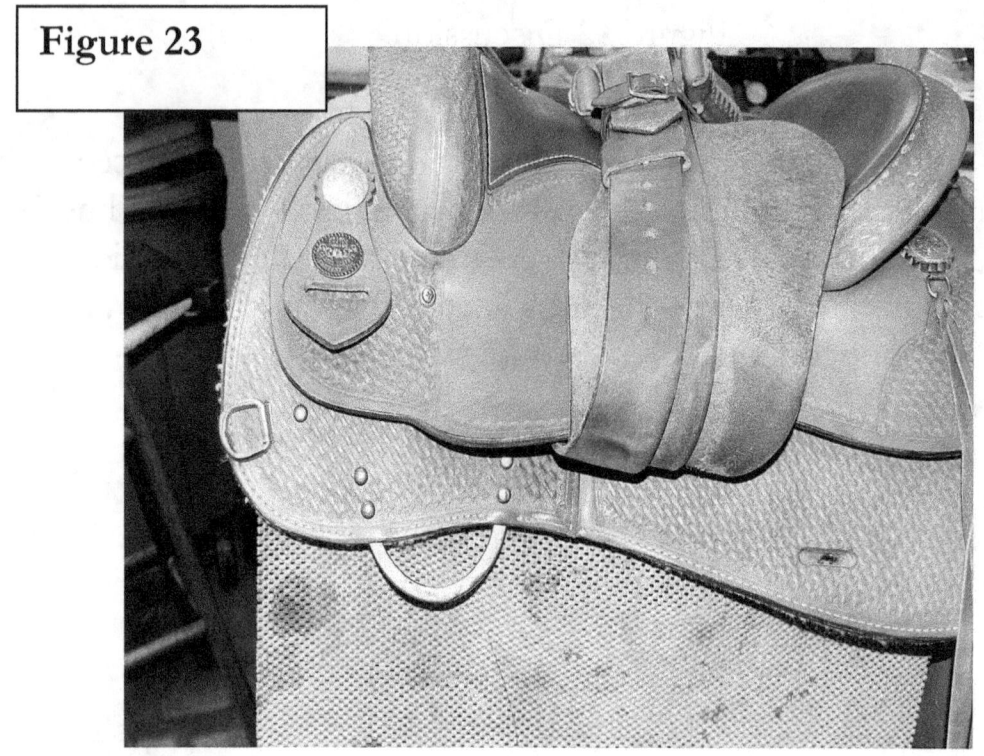

Figure 23

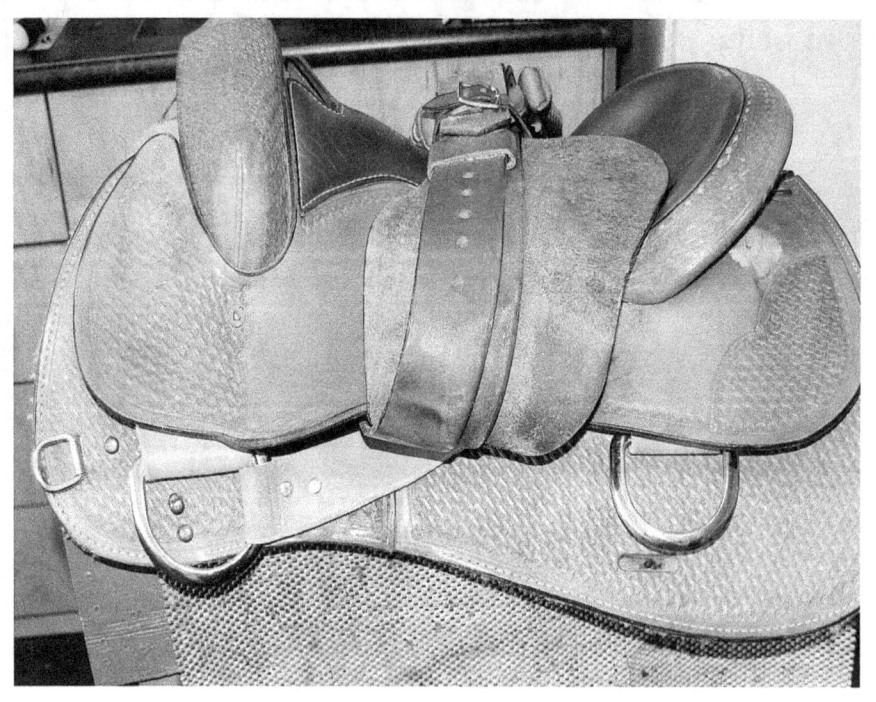

Figure 23 Discussion

Left Top - an in-skirt single nickel plated ring in the 7/8 position. Note the curved edge at the bottom of the skirting. This prevents the placement of a three-way in-skirt rigging.

Left Bottom - Here the in-skirt rigging has been replaced with a Stohlman Standard D type rigging in the full position. Note how the old holes have been filled in with rivets for cosmetic purposes.

With In-skirt to Standard Style, the conchos have to be temporarily removed and the tie strings undone, if they exist, to expose the base of the fork and at the rear of the tree. Screws and nails under the conchos also have to be removed. In a double rig, the rear jockey will have to be taken off. More information is included in the Appendix on how to disassemble saddles.

Single Brass Plate to a Three-way Brass In-skirt

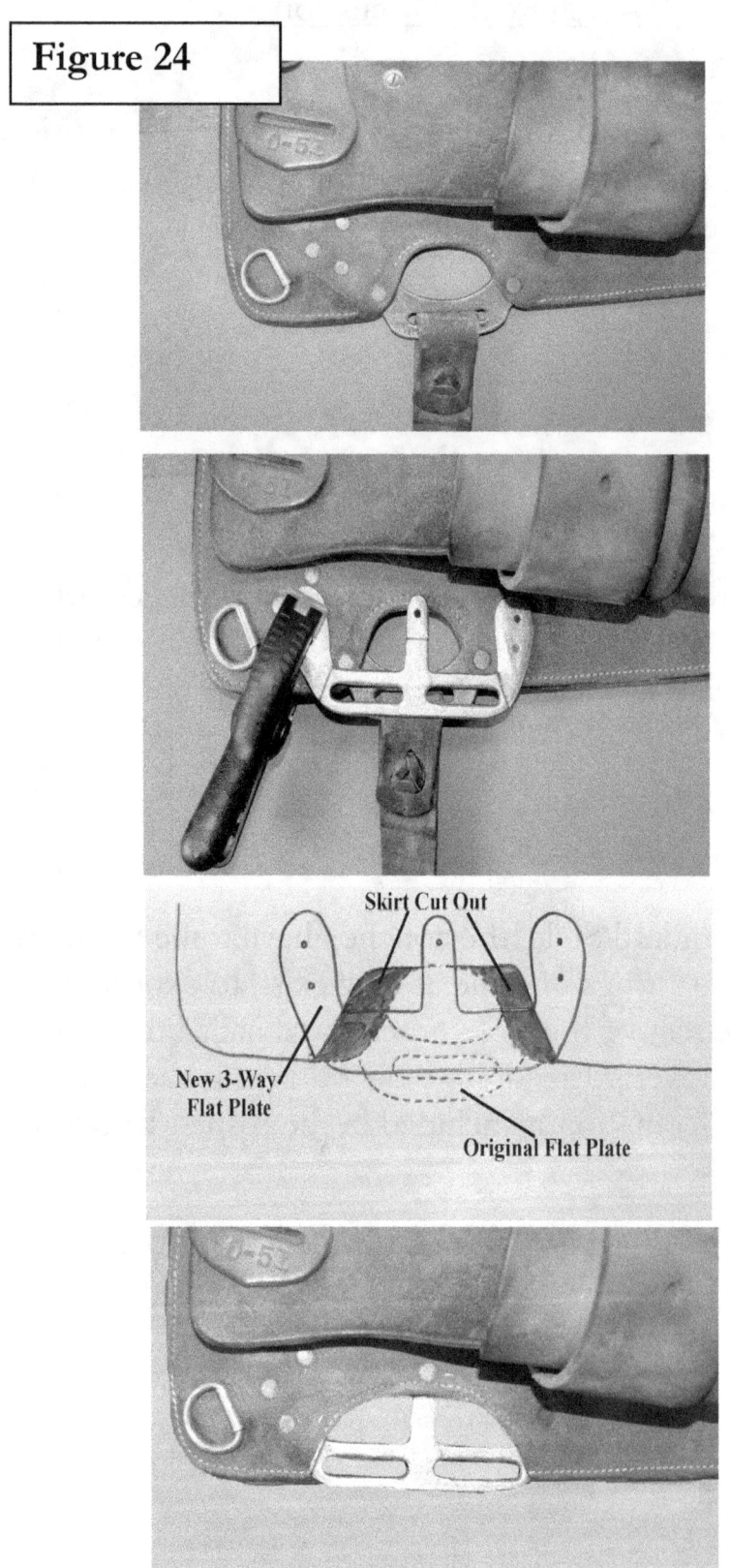

Figure 24

46

Figure 24 Discussion

Left Top - Brass plate in-skirt rigging in 7/8 position. Note the hole that was cut in the skirting to accommodate this type of rigging.

Left Top Center - Here a brass three-way rig has been placed over the existing in-skirt rigging for comparison and fitting. Planning where the rivet holes will be placed is an important step.

Left Bottom Center - You should always draw out your modifications first on cardboard. Here the original skirting outline and single plated rig are drawn superimposed with the new three-way plate. The shaded areas indicate where the skirt needs to be further cut with a utility knife to install the new three-way rig. Cut out the shaded areas of the cardboard and trace these on the saddle skirting; then cut this area out of the skirting.

Left Bottom - Here the new three-way plate rigging has been installed. Note the new cutouts in the skirt. Re-sewing the skirting is optional as long as the skirting layers are glued back together sufficiently.

Single Brass Hanging Plate to a Three-way Brass Plate Rigging.

Figure 25

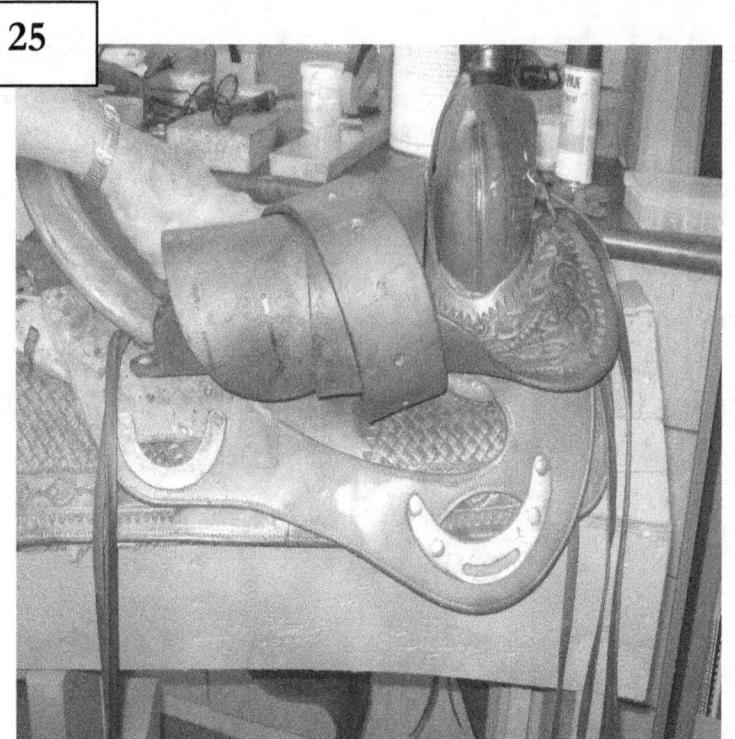

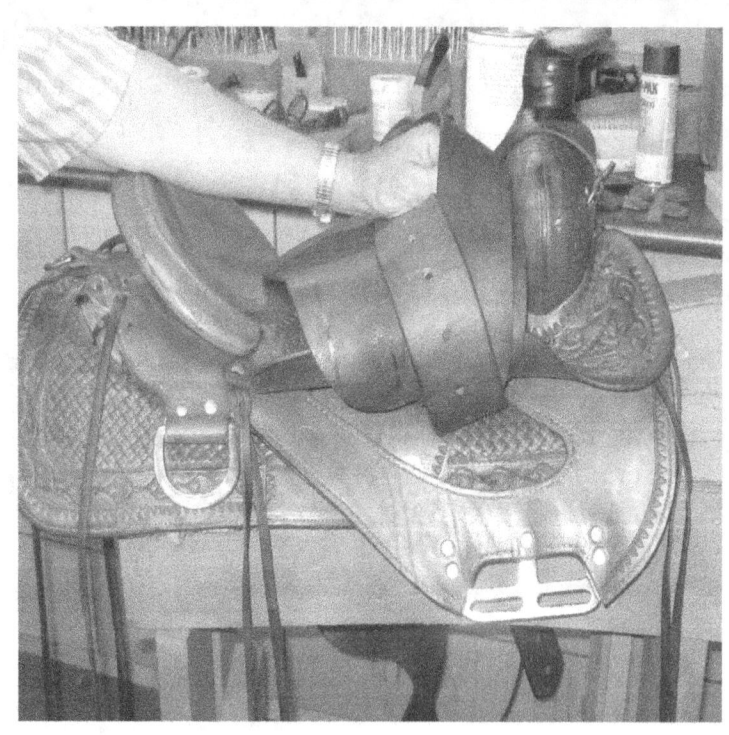

Figure 25 Discussion

Left Top - This shows a hanging plate rigging in the 7/8 position. This saddle was bridging in this position. It placed the rider too far forward and made the horse sore.

Left Bottom - Here the hanging plate and entire leather rigging has been replaced with a flat plate three-way. The hanging rigging leathers are double thickness for strength and sandwiches in the three-way plate ends. Although time consuming, this procedure is not too difficult, but you should have access to a sewing machine or be prepared to hand stitch the double thickness leathers.

Hanging plate 7/8 position to Full Position Standard

Figure 26

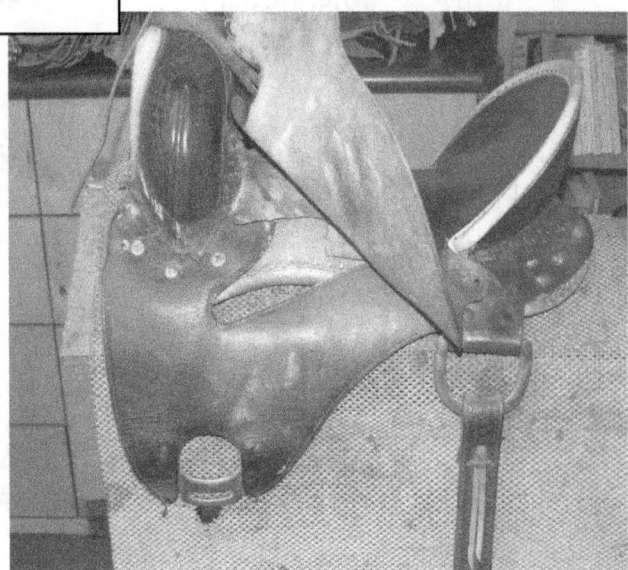

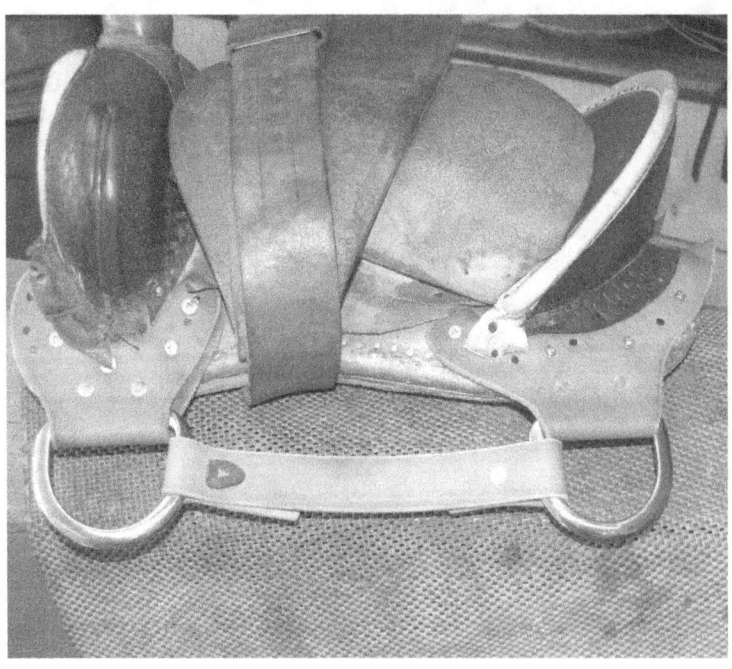

Figure 26 Discussion

Left Top - In this example, a 7/8 hanging plate rig has been modified to a full position Standard Double D configuration. For clarity, the skirts of the saddle in this example have been removed but this would not have been required.

Left Bottom - Note the addition of both front and rear Ds. Only the jockeys would have had to be temporarily removed. The swell cover (pommel) edges have been lifted and placed over the new leathers for cosmetic reasons only. Other than 3/4 inch carpet tacks to hold the new leathers temporarily in place, sheet metal or wood screws are used (#14 x 1 1/4) to secure the mounting. Avoid using nails as they will tend to split the wood in the tree. The rear leather riggings use #10 x 1 screws.

Single In-skirt D to Three-way Jump Rigging

Figure 27

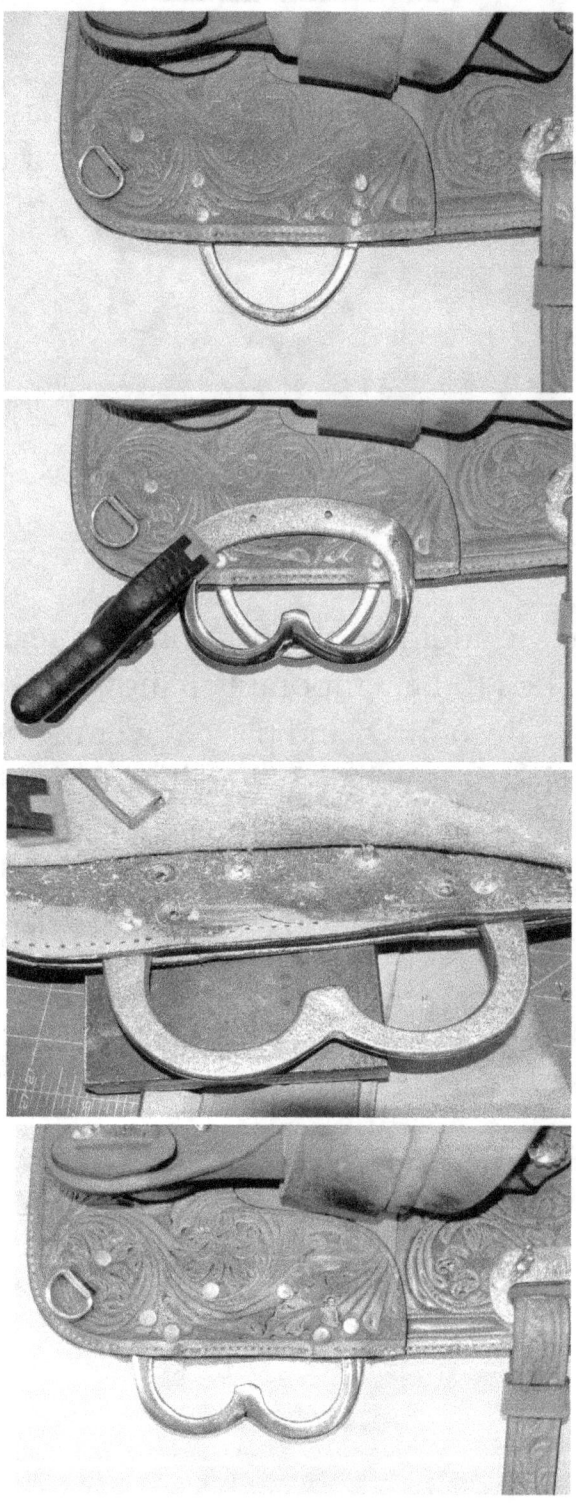

Figure 27 Discussion

Left Top - Shown is a typical in-skirt rigging in the 7/8 position. Note that the skirts do not have to be removed to modify this configuration.

Left Top Center - Here a three-way jump rigging has been placed over the single in-skirt rigging. The three-way jump rigging allows billets or latigos to be positioned without untying or re-rigging.

Left Bottom Center- Under-view of new three-way jump rig which has been sandwiched between the skirting leathers. Note how the shearling has been pulled back. This will later be glued back down.

Left Bottom - Completed installation of new rigging. Note the old rivet holes have been filled for cosmetic purposes.

Modifying Rock of Bars

This type of modification is more technical and requires a little more know-how of saddle construction and a few more tools. You may have to seek some help from your local saddle maker for this step if you are unsure how to proceed. For modifications of the rock of the bars, the saddle has to be disassembled to expose the underside of the bars. Instructions for disassembly of a saddle are included in the Appendix.

The diagram in Figure 28 shows the conceptual building up of the bars with leather strips. The leather strips can be cut with a utility knife around the edges and then skived or rasped to a smooth arc. Be sure to make the built-up portions at the rear of the bars flat across the width. Note the original saddle tree stirrup slots have been filled in with a leather filler.

Figure 28 - Detail of Cross Section of Bar Filler

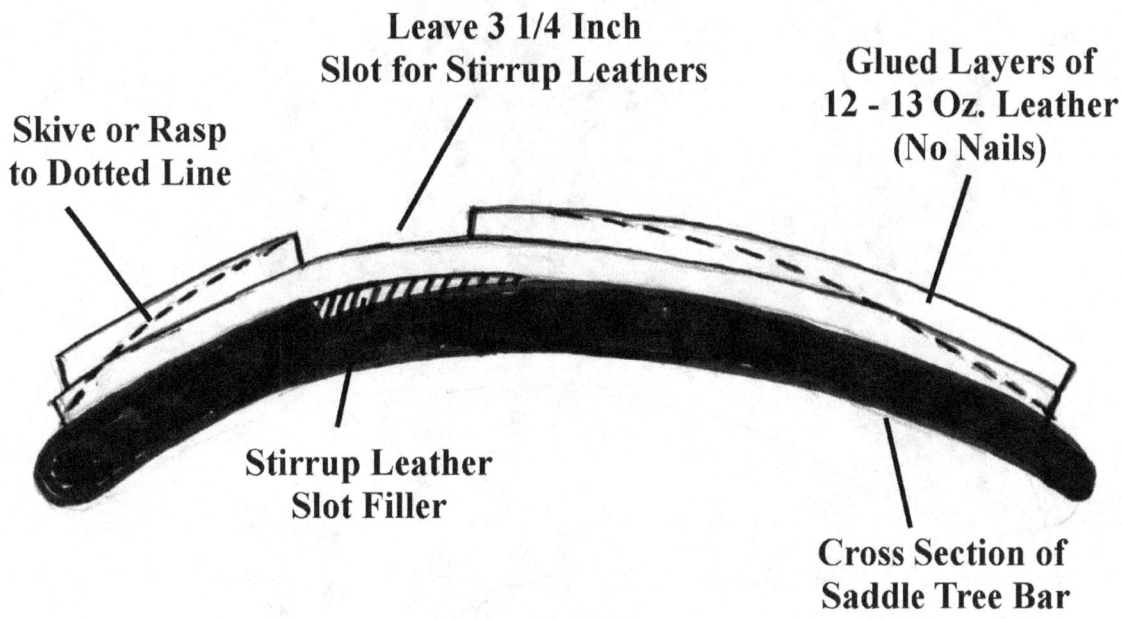

No nails are used in the entire operation. All layers are glued together and glued to the tree bars. The saddle tree can be returned to its original rock later by simple clasping the glued-on layers with a pair of pliers and pulling them off. Figures 29 thru 31 illustrate examples of how to determine the area of the bars that need to be built up and techniques to accomplish this.

Figure 29

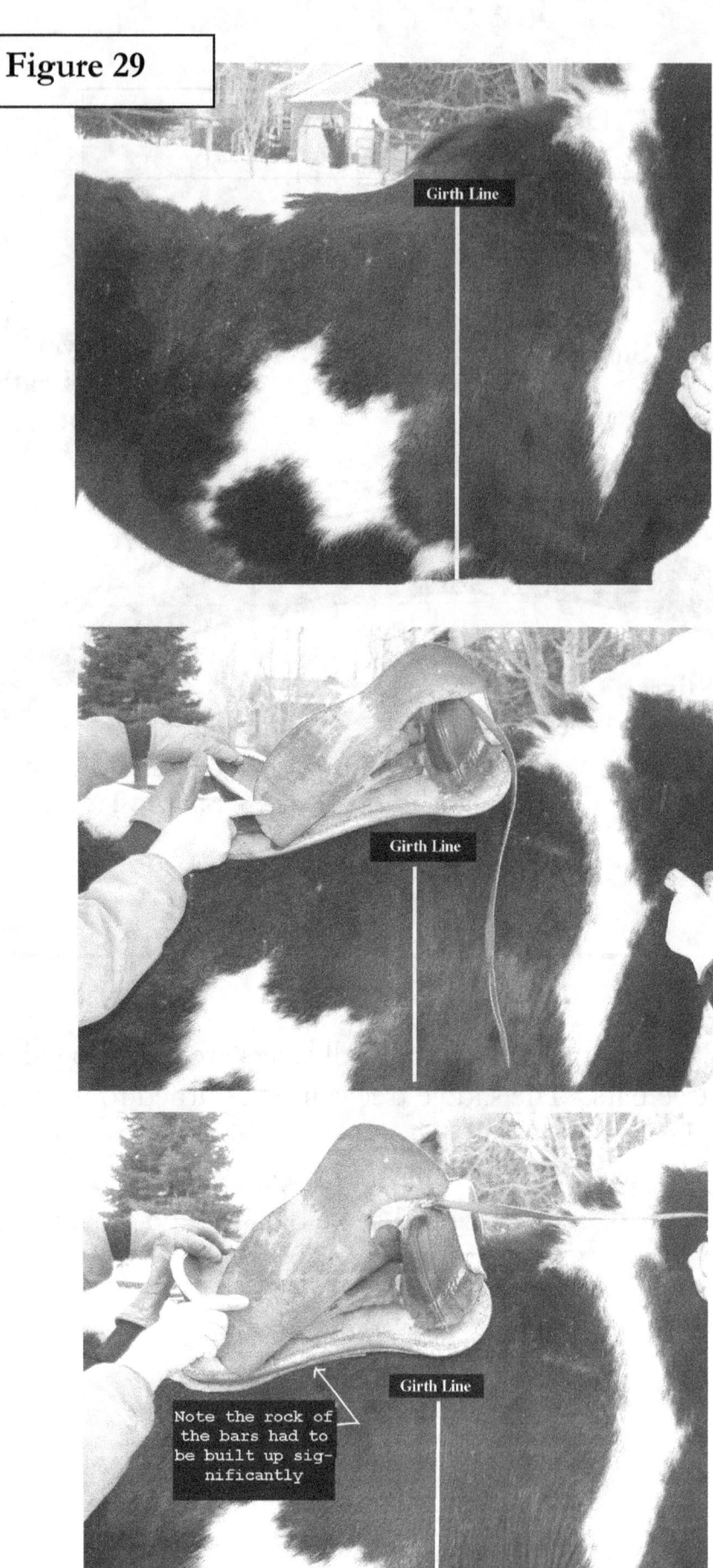

Figure 29 Discussion

Left Top - Here we have a very high withered horse which was getting sore when ridden. The saddle had a 7/8 rigging position. Note the girth line in white.

Left Middle - After removing the skirts from the saddle, it became apparent that a large amount of bridging was occurring. The horse also had significant sores over the kidney area where the back ends of the saddle bars were digging in.

Left Bottom - After trying the rigging at the full position, bridging was reduced but there was still a significant gap between the bars and the horse's back. As a result, this saddle was modified to the full-rigging position, and then fillers were glued in under the bars to increase the rock.

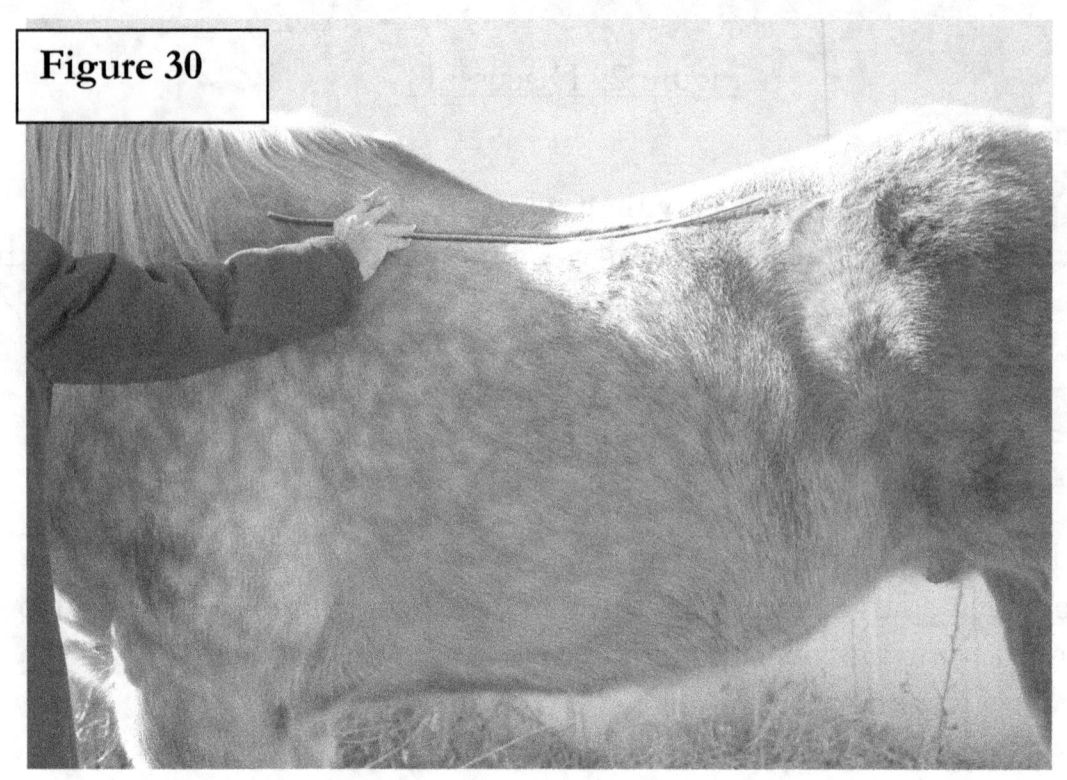

Figure 30

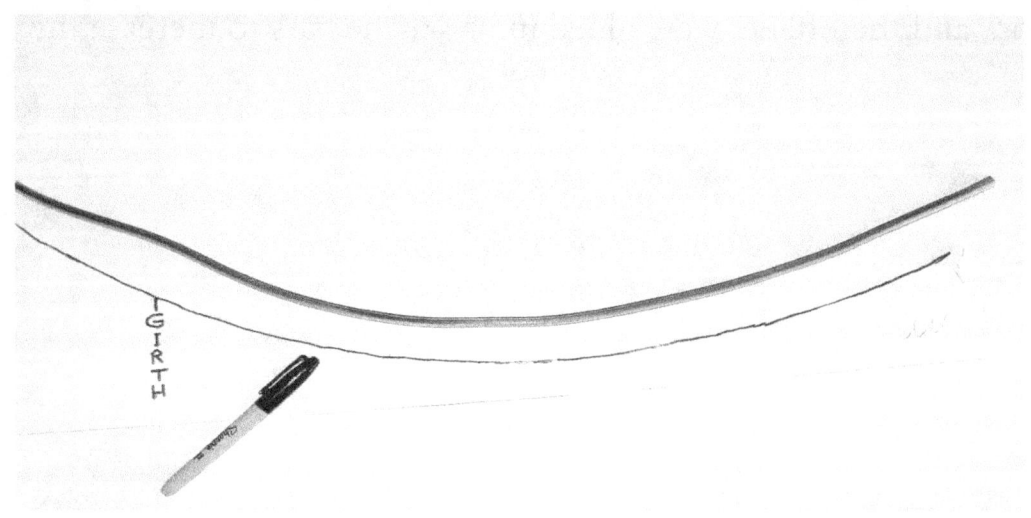

Figure 30 Discussion

Left Top - When the rock of the bars need to be modified, place a stiff wire or a flexible engineering tape (shown) along the back of the horse where the bars are positioned. Be sure to mark the girth position. The position of the flexible tape shows where the saddle tree bar should contact the horse. The difference between this layout and the existing saddle bar rock is where the bars need to be built up.

Left Bottom - The flexible tape is placed on cardboard, and then traced. A cut-out is made along the line to form a template for building up the bar area. Note the girth mark which must align with the rigging position of the saddle tree.

Figure 31

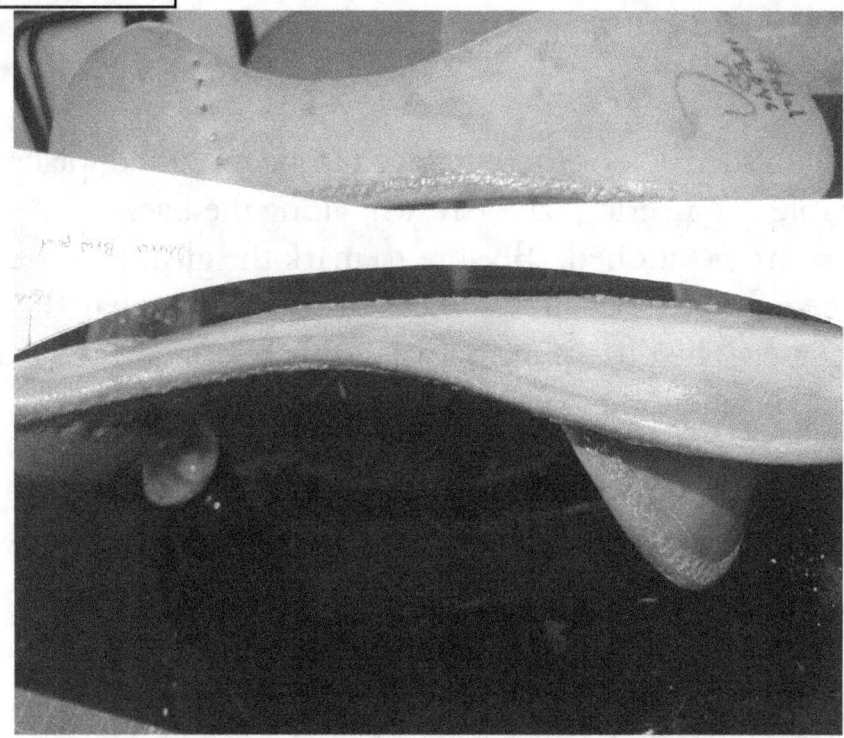

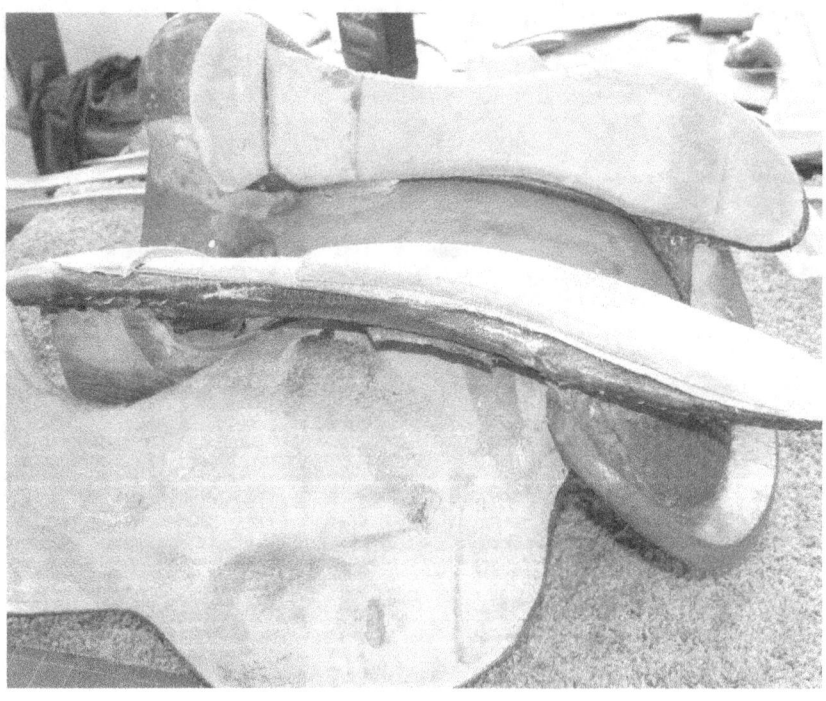

Figure 31 Discussion

Left Top - Here the template made in the previous step is placed over the bars. Note that the saddle skirts have been removed. Place the tree on the horse to assure that the rigging is positioned correctly and that the bar build-up will be satisfactory. It is better to under-build rather than over-build the bar rock. Use the cardboard template as a guide for how much the rock of the bars is to be built up. Leather is glued to the bars in layers and then the outer edges trimmed with a utility knife. Never nail leather to the bars because the nails may work loose.

Left Bottom - Here the new leather over the bars is shown trimmed and skived down. Use a rasp or skiving knife for this purpose. Note that slots for the stirrup leathers have been left as recesses just as with the original tree bars. Try the tree on the horse periodically while the skiving is in process so that a "best fit" can be obtained.

Conclusion

For more than a century, the western saddle has been the cowboy's most important tool; and his horse has been his best friend and companion. How well the two go together can lead to harmony or bad experiences.

Hopefully, some thoughts and ideas have been presented in the foregoing chapters that will allow the readers to evaluate the fit of their saddles and possibly apply some remedies to correct problems.

APPENDIX

    A. How to Disassemble a Saddle

    B. Patterns for Standard Front and Rear Riggings

    C. Where to Purchase 3-way Rigging

Appendix A - How to Disassemble a Saddle

Saddle disassembly can be very easy on a well-constructed saddle and difficult for even an experienced saddle maker on a poorly or cheaply constructed saddle. Basically, the skirts are held onto the bars by screws and nails. Some saddles also have saddle strings that pass through the bars and skirts and then tied on top of the jockeys. A properly-constructed saddle will never have nails passing through the shearling or sheepskin to hold the skirts in place, except for four or five screws or nails in the gullet. Reference Figures 32 and 33.

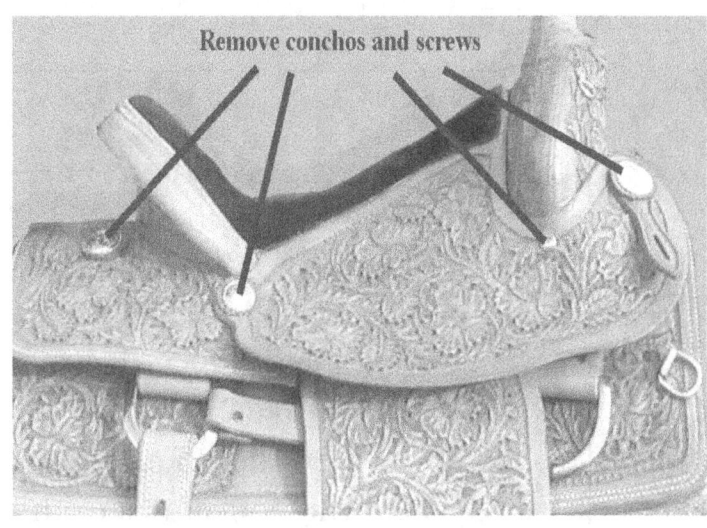

Figure 32

Left Top - Start first by removing the conchos and the fork screw. There will be nails and screws under the conchos that will need to be removed also.

Tight conchos can be broke loose by tapping the edge with a screw driver and hammer in a counter-clock wise direction.

The rear jockey can now be removed.

Left Bottom - There will be four or five nails and/or screws in the gullet at the top of the skirt. Remove these.

As a word of caution, some cheaper and lighter constructed-saddles may contain a thin masonite rather than leather for the inside lining of the skirts. Because glues will not adhere to this material, the shearlings or sheepskins are often attached by pneumatic nail guns. It is not uncommon to find a dozen or more nails per side holding the skirt to the under bars. Collared nails are often used with this type of construction, so the only way to remove them from the bars is to cut them off with a pair of nippers. With these saddles, the masonite should be replaced with leather to allow the bars to conform to the horse's back and glue used to hold the shearling to the under skirt.

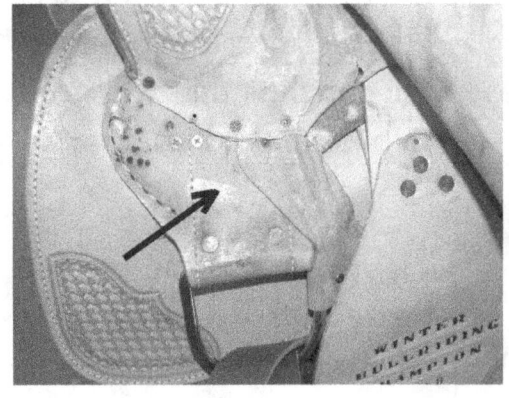

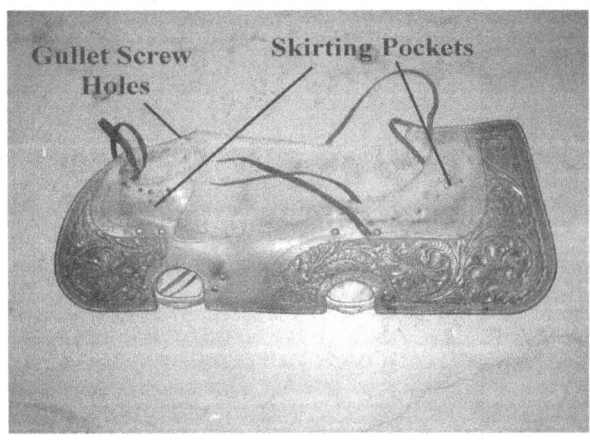

Figure 33

Left Top - Skirts are held onto the bars by pockets or leather straps called lugs in both the front and rear of the bars. Undo the screws and nails holding these in place. The swell cover may have to be rolled up a bit on the bottom to access where the pocket ties to the tree. On standard-rigged saddles, it is common to find the rigging leathers sewn to the skirt and also functioning as a pocket for the front end of the bars. (Arrow)

Left Bottom - A skirt removed from the saddle tree showing front and rear pockets and the holes from the gullet screws.

Once the skirts are removed, the bars should be fully exposed. It is not necessary to remove the swell cover, seat, or cantle covering. After modification, saddles should be reassembled with screws.

Appendix B - Patterns for Standard Front and Rear Riggings

On the following patterns, each square equals one square inch. The front rigging is on the top and the rear rig is on the bottom. It is a good idea to place a section of nylon belt webbing around the base of the rigging D for added wear strength. Be sure to soak the leather before bending to avoid cracking and weakening and slightly skive or taper the ends where they attach under the fork or pommel. Attach the front rigging to the bars with #14 x 1 1/4 sheet metal screws and the rear rigging with #10x1 or #10 x 1 1/4 sheet metal screws. Copper rivets are needed on the rear rig after completing the fold.

Figure 34

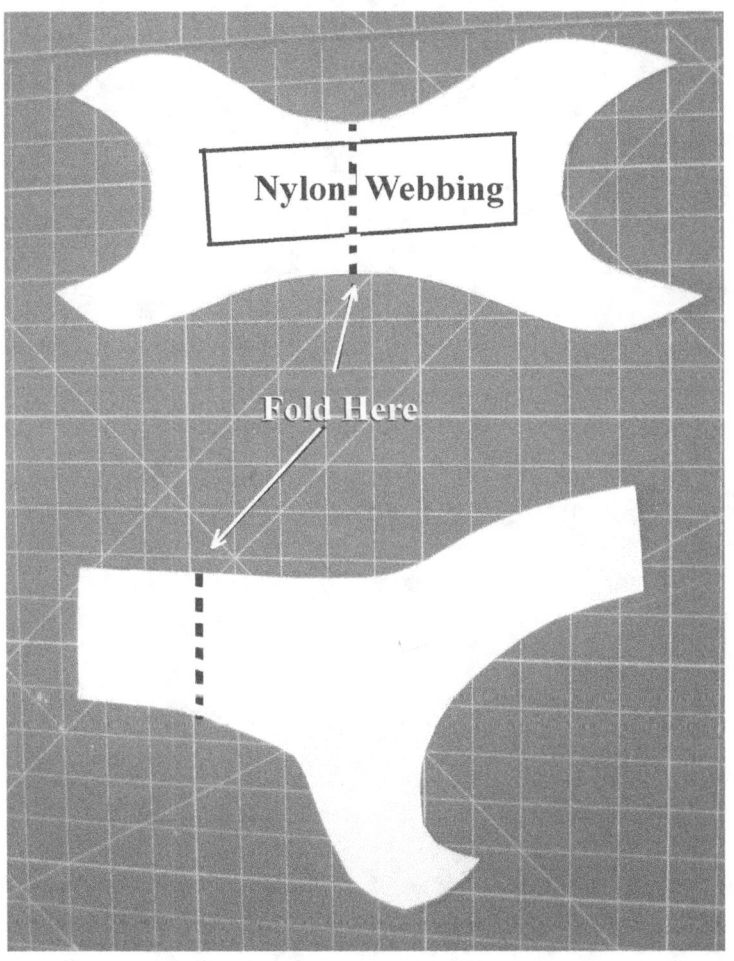

Appendix C - Where to Purchase 3-way Riggings

Nickel Plated

Tandy - Leather Factory Stores Nationwide

Brass Plated

Bork Saddlery Hardware
823 W. 2nd St.
Pendleton, OR 97801
541-276-5207

The Boise Foundry
PO Box 34
221 Carrie Rex
Melba, ID 83641
208-495-1220

About the Author:

David Prevedel has been a saddle maker for over 15 years, specializing in custom hand-made saddles and equestrian gear. He is considered a saddle historian having restored scores of vintage saddles dating from the late 1880's to the 1920s, and has an extensive personal collection of antique saddles.

Dave also conducts seminars on saddle fitting. He owns and operates Prevedel Saddlery located in Hooper, Utah and can be reached at 801-985-2437.

Also visit us at: www.prevedelsaddlery.com

www.ingramcontent.com/pod-product-compliance
Lightning Source LLC
Chambersburg PA
CBHW080820170526

45158CB00009B/2482